The Connection Codes have truly changed our lives- we use the tools every day! It has been absolutely beautiful and amazing to see how much stronger our connection with each other and our kids has become.

Seth and Lauren Dahl, Austin TX

The Connection Code tools have been absolutely revolutionary in our leadership, marriage, and parenting. The journey has been incredible. We cannot say enough about how they have impacted us. Share this book with everyone you know!

Shawn & Michelle Gabie, Ottawa Canada

Everyone needs the Connection Codes! It opens up a whole new world of intimacy and connection we never knew existed! We talk Connection Code with everyone now like it's a second language.

Jalila Hudson, Nashville TN

For years we struggled with our communication and emotions- we began to think it would never get easier. Then we learned the Connection Codes tools and they've changed our marriage, friendships and life. This is the best investment we've ever made!

Miriam & Michael Strand, Kalisz Poland

The Connection Codes have brought about a deep inner healing and a sense of power in my life that I did not have before. Thank you!

Lana Cruz, Redding CA

The practical and profound tools of the Connection Codes have changed our lives! The benefits are HUGE and it has been an utter joy and delight getting to know Connection Coders around the world!

Claire & Luke Farman, West Sussex England

We did the Connection Codes fundamentals and parenting class and our home has been transformed. Thank you so much for these tools- they are changing our lives!

Jennifer, Spring Hill TN

The Connection Codes have been a gamechanger! As a result, I have recently reunited with a sibling who hasn't communicated with me for decades. I am so grateful for this series- it is life-changing, and I thoroughly recommend it to everyone!

Gay Hartley, Melbourne Australia

As someone who grew up in the church and has had every kind of inner healing/heart healing/generational healing, etc you can think of, something was always missing. I so appreciate that the connection code is taught from a psychological and scientific perspective, not just a blanketed, ultra-spiritualized and sensationalized sentiment.

Bethany, Chicago IL

The Connection Codes have transformed our marriage, our parenting and all our relationships. These tools have given us what we need to maintain healthy connections with our teenagers and pass on the ability to communicate and connect deeply. We use the Connection Codes every day without exception.

Leslie Biehn, Stratford Ontario

The unique piece the Connection Codes brings to our family's wholeness puzzle has been sorely missing and the felt relief of its discovery is no less than profound! Our entire understanding of relationships has shifted in a way it never had before!

Chandler Jo, Oklahoma

We've spent a small fortune on marriage and family counseling and have never made so much progress so quickly. So simple, implementable and powerful! Thank you!!

The Kohlers, Zurich Switzerland

After 20 years of marriage, the Connection Codes have been life changing! We love the freedom we've found to connect deeply. We've been given renewed hope to have an incredible marriage.

Laura Pimentel, Sacramento CA

I don't want to be vulnerable until I know you're safe, but I won't know you're safe until I'm vulnerable. Also, I don't offer safety until you're vulnerable, but you won't want to be vulnerable until you know I'm safe. So, someone has to take a risk.

The Connection Codes

THE BLUEPRINT & TOOLS FOR CREATING THE RELATIONSHIPS YOU CRAVE

Dr Glenn & Phyllis Hill
with Echo Hill-Vetter

The Connection Codes: The relational blueprint and tools for emotional healing and building the connections you crave

Copyright © 2021 Dr Glenn Hill

All rights reserved. No part of this book may be reproduced or used in any manner without the prior written permission of the copyright owner, except for the use of brief quotations in a book review.

To request permissions, contact the publisher at connectioncodes@drglennhill.com

ISBN: 978-1-7376500-0-3

connectioncodes.co

*This is dedicated to everyone in pursuit of
the deep connection that makes life worth living.*

Contents

Introduction xv

SECTION 1
Identity 1

SECTION 2
Emotion: A Human Right 53

SECTION 3
Core Emotion Wheel 99

SECTION 4
The Cycle 147

SECTION 5
Relationship Science 169

Conclusion & Beginning 189

We were together.
I forget the rest.

If you love deeply, you hurt deeply. If you don't, it's much worse.

Humans are the least likely species on the planet to survive independently.

Here are pictures of some one-year-olds.

Who would you pick in a race? Who would you pick in a fight? Who would you pick to survive? How old do humans have to be to survive on their own? Two years old, four, seven? Most species are fully functional within months of birth. We are *by far* the slowest maturing and least viable species on the planet.

BUT

Humans are the *most* likely species not just to survive but to thrive *inter*dependently. We are coded from birth for relationship, for connection, for tandemship, for functioning interdependently with each other.

Problem: most of us do not know how to live interdependently.

SO

Welcome to the Connection Codes! We are thrilled you are here and embarking on a journey that will transform your relationships and enrich your life!

Many of us do not believe we are worthy of experiencing connection, safety and love. As Stephen Chbosky said in *The Perks of Being a Wallflower,* "We accept the love we think we deserve."

Our desire is to be a gentle voice screaming in your ear that you *are* worthy of experiencing connection; you *deserve* to be loved.

A FEW ♪'S AS WE BEGIN:

♪ The Connection Codes preexisted us. We did not invent them; we simply swept them into a pile and labeled them. They are the blueprint of how humans connect in relationship, as well as a set of tools for facilitating that process. They are the culmination of over 30 years of research, education and experience. In actuality, they are the culmination of far more, as they are built on the efforts and insights of innumerable people over many centuries.

♪ Each of us is coded, or hardwired, for relational connection with other humans. The goal is to reactivate that coding. You do not need to learn it; you need to *re*learn it. You do not need to learn a *new* language; this is the language of your birth.

♪ Psychology is a soft science. When you combine 2 particles of hydrogen with 1 particle of oxygen, you get water. You always get water, you never get cotton candy, a shoe or a new car (unfortunately). You do not have to replicate that formula endlessly to determine if it is accurate. That is 'hard' science. It is dependable because every particle of hydrogen is the same as every other particle of hydrogen. The same is true of oxygen. This is not true of humans. Each human is unique and complex, and we must keep this in mind when examining human behavior. Humans are bad lab rats, which makes it difficult to determine how an individual will function. Thus, we must be discerning as we apply general concepts to specific people and relationships.

♪ The Connection Codes are based on the fundamental human condition and experience. While we the authors have a faith-based heritage, the Connection Codes are not presented from a faith-based perspective. Whether the human condition is evolutionary or a Creator's design, the result is the same. As with gravity, the Connection Codes apply to every human, whether faith-based or otherwise.

♪ The Connection Codes are experiential, not just conceptual. The power is not in the knowledge; the power is in the relational interaction. Experience Assignments are included at the end of each section to help apply these concepts.

♪ The Connection Codes are a puzzle. When working a puzzle, you may look at a particular piece and think it doesn't belong with this puzzle (one of the risks of buying puzzles at yard sales). Then, when the puzzle is completed, it is obvious the piece *does* fit.

Some Connection Codes' puzzle pieces may seem that way, but as you process the content and do the Experience Assignments, the picture will become clear.

This is a simple process; it is not an easy one. Returning to your original coding may be the most challenging thing you ever do. It will also be the most rewarding.

You need this.
You deserve this.
Let's do this!

SECTION 1
Identity

The #1, fundamental, foundational, most pressing human need is not food, water or oxygen. We can go without food for weeks. We can go without water for days. We can go without oxygen for minutes. Each of these can occur without damage.

> *The Guiness Book of World Records reports Aleix Segura Vendrell held his breath for 24 minutes 3.45 seconds in 2016!*

The #1, fundamental, foundational, most pressing human need is Identity. We cannot go without Identity for very many seconds without experiencing harm, sometimes extreme and lasting levels of harm.

What do we mean by Identity? We receive Identity when we get yes answers to questions such as:

Do I exist?	*Do I exist to you?*
Do I matter?	*Do I matter to you?*
Do I have value and significance?	*Do I have value and significance to you?*
Am I good enough?	*Am I good enough for you?*

We lose Identity if we don't get yes answers to those questions.

CONSIDER

You are at a party and are introduced to Fred. You greet him and extend your hand to shake his. He looks at you but does not return your greeting nor extend his hand to shake yours.

How long before you begin to feel uncomfortable? How long before you feel the need to move away from Fred?

You are losing Identity. You are getting the message from Fred that you do not exist; you do not matter; you do not have value; you are not good enough. Very quickly, you start thinking, "Hmmm, I believe I'll go find someone else to talk to." Being with Fred becomes undesirable because you are losing Identity, and you will not (cannot) connect with Fred.

Every human is born with the need for Identity, the pressing need to know, "I matter." The Dalai Lama calls it self-esteem or self-confidence; Brene Brown calls it self-worth; Dale Carnegie calls it a sense of being important. This is coded within each of us from birth. We do not plan it and often are not aware of it; the need is innate. We connect with people from whom we receive Identity. We are coded to move toward those people. We do not connect with people from whom we do not receive Identity, particularly if we lose Identity. We are coded to move away from those people.

The need for Identity is not good or bad, right or wrong; it simply is. As with food, water or oxygen, we do not endeavor to permanently eliminate those needs. We do not think in terms of someday maturing to the point of no longer needing them. No one attempts to breathe sufficiently this month so as not to need to breathe next month. No one will be able to hydrate enough this year so as not to need liquid intake next year. In the same way, the need for Identity is ongoing.

When we grasp the significance of Identity, we see more clearly the effect we can have on another person's experience, on another person's life. Identity is sometimes used as a verb, such as, "I felt special when she Identitied me" or "I feel so valued when he Identities me."

IDENTITY METER

We would like to invent an Identity meter. This would be worn on the wrist so that both people in an interaction could read it. It would serve to let both people know what is happening at the core. Thus, people would know when Identity is being received or lost. Something like:

> *"Oh wow, your Identity meter spiked. You just received Identity! I want to know what happened, so it can be repeated in the future."*
>
> **OR**
>
> *"Oh my, your Identity meter dropped. You just lost Identity! I want to know what happened, so hopefully, it won't be repeated in the future."*
>
> **OR**
>
> *"Hey, I just received Identity from what you said. That felt really good. Thanks!"*
>
> **OR**
>
> *"Ugh, I just lost some Identity when you did that. That was kinda tough for me."*

Most of us are unaware of the gain or loss of Identity for ourselves or others. Thus, interactions frequently cause disconnect without one or both parties realizing what happened to bring about that disconnect. Most conflicts originate with a loss of Identity by one or more parties.

The first step in reactivating your coding for connection is to become aware of Identity. This will be from one of four angles: you receiving or losing Identity or the other person receiving or losing Identity. When one of these occurs, you can convey that to the other person in the interaction. If they are a Connection Coder, they will get it and be present with you. If they are not a Connection Coder, it will make for some interesting conversation while introducing them to the Connection Codes!

Additionally, you can become aware of assisting others with their #1, fundamental, foundational, most pressing human need;

you can become aware of Identitying another person. There are countless ways this can be done, but it may be as simple as a friendly greeting, especially if you add a smile.

Another important point concerning Identity is that the gain or loss of Identity has more significance in some relationships than in others, particularly those that are long term. While it feels awful being treated with disregard by the grocery store cashier, it probably will have limited effect. Being treated with disregard by a relative can have a severe, long lasting effect. Some people struggle every day because of the loss of Identity they experienced in childhood. Many marriages suffer because one or both parties experience loss of Identity.

Nevertheless, at times, there are severe repercussions from a brief encounter where someone lost Identity. The news is full of stories of a horrific action someone took in reaction to losing Identity. Road rage is a prime example; someone gets cut off in traffic and receives a message from the other of, "You don't matter. You have no significance. You are not worth my consideration." Most of us have seen altercations between two strangers over something seemingly trivial. Often, the driving force behind the conflict is a loss of Identity for one or both parties. They then respond out of a sense of desperation, which can produce harrowing results.

On an encouraging note, Identity can be re-established quickly. One Identity bringing interaction can begin connection for a relationship that has been in disarray. Just as one breath is tremendously reassuring and stabilizing for someone who has been without oxygen, one Identity bringing interaction with a significant other can be tremendously reassuring and stabilizing.

HI

Phyllis:

I was walking down a long hallway in an office building and saw a little boy sitting toward the side of the walkway. Several other people were walking ahead of me and as each passed, the little guy looked up at them. Each person was engrossed in thought or discussion, and none of them looked at the child. As I approached and he looked at me, I smiled at him. He instantly smiled back and said, "Hi."

He automatically responded even though he had never seen me before. He did not think this through; it was an automatic reaction. Because I conveyed to him that he had value, he wanted to connect with me. I'm not criticizing the other adults. They were engaged in thoughts, conversations or activities. Nonetheless, the little boy did not receive Identity from them, thus he did not connect.

LET ME TELL YOU ABOUT ME
(P.S. I DON'T CARE ABOUT YOU)

Glenn:

We went on a cruise with a large group of extended family, many of whom we previously had not met. On the first day, I talked with a middle-aged man for about half an hour. He told me his life story with extensive details about where he had been and what he had done. I listened attentively and asked questions concerning his narrative. He did not ask questions about me or my life. I was ok with that and happy to get to know him, although I walked away with an odd, empty feeling.

The next day, I saw him again, and he continued his narrative. As before, I listened and engaged, and as before, he asked no questions about me. Again, I walked away with an odd, empty feeling.

The third day, the same process began again, but we were interrupted by someone making an announcement. I experienced a sense of relief as he engaged with someone else after the announcement.

The fourth day, I entered the room where the group was meeting, and the same man was standing directly in front of me! I experienced a visceral feeling and noticed my body turning away from him to engage with someone, anyone else. I felt my body actively resisting interacting with that person. My body seemed to be directing itself not to be in a non-Identitying situation.

I'm not judging the other man in this story. I was simply fascinated by the physiological experience of my body resisting a non-Identity bringing interaction.

Identity is why people are drawn to good listeners. A good listener conveys: "You exist. You matter. You are worthy of my attention. I am interested in you." This gives Identity, which creates interest for the speaker to pursue connection with the listener.

A POWERFUL LITTLE FINGER

Glenn:

At an event attended by several hundred people, I saw a woman I had not seen in many years. She was with her husband, whom I had never met. Both of them were extremely overweight and moved slowly, the husband requiring two canes to get around. She introduced us, whereupon the husband immediately declared, "I could kill anyone in this room with my little finger." Recognizing his deep craving for Identity, I listened. He went on to explain that he had been in the Marines forty years prior and spoke longingly of that experience.

After the ceremony, I extended an invitation for them to stay with us if they were ever in our area. Giving no response to the invitation, he said, "I accomplished more in the Marines than anyone here has in their entire life." I did not know how he knew the accomplishment level of each of the several hundred people in attendance, but I nodded, added a "Wow!" and bid them farewell. As I left, I pondered the deep pain and longing he must experience to solicit Identity so aggressively.

MOM, WATCH THIS!

Echo:

Understanding the importance of Identity has affected my marriage immeasurably. Over the years, my husband has described the joy he experiences when I greet him when he gets home from work. He has also communicated the sadness he feels when that greeting is absent. Being aware of Identity helps me to be mindful to greet him, even if I am tired or distracted. Even briefly Identitying each other brings connection and changes the trajectory of our entire evening. This awareness has transformed our moments and, thus, our lives.

Also, Identity is why my children will say, "Mom, watch this!" dozens of times every day. What they are conveying is, "Mom, I need you to give me Identity! Mom, connect with me!" My children look to me for Identity throughout the day, every day. I give them Identity when I regard what they are showing or telling me. My attention communicates to them: You exist; you matter; you have value; you are enough.

Lawrence (Connection Coder):

I had attended a Connection Codes workshop, was enthralled with the concepts and determined to implement them. The next day, I was at a work conference, and the Identity idea came to mind. I determined I would peruse the room, find someone who looked like they were lacking Identity and talk with them. I saw someone standing alone who struck me as feeling left out, so I approached him and began a conversation. As we conversed, I endeavored to make certain he was receiving Identity.

> *It turned out that the individual who had been standing alone was a coordinator of Ted Talks, and at the end of the conversation, he asked if I would be interested in giving a Ted Talk! While this was not my goal in seeking to Identity someone, my experience has been that some remarkable things can happen when we Identity another human.*

DISREGARD = DISREGARD

Upon grasping the magnitude of Identity, one might think, "I would never do anything to cause someone to lose Identity- that would be terrible." Nonetheless, we often do this very thing.

If you disregard a person's experience, you disregard the person. Conversely, if you regard a person's experience, you regard the person. We often think those can be separated, but they cannot.

CONSIDER

> Your little girl comes running to you and excitedly says, "Look, I made this picture for you!" You look at the picture, turn it at different angles and say, "I can't even tell what this is. It doesn't look like anything to me." You wad it up, throw it in the trash, turn back to the child and say, "But, I care about *you!*"

Although you said you care about her, your daughter will not believe you. You disregarded her experience of drawing the picture and showing it to you, thus you disregarded her. She will catalog your disregard of her experience as disregard for her. She will catalog that you do not care about her and, thus, will be less inclined to share her experience with you in the future.

In this scenario, your daughter is losing Identity. She feels she does not matter to you because her experience does not seem to matter to you. She feels she is not valued by you because her experience does not seem valued by you. She feels she is not good enough for you because her experience does not seem good enough for you.

The same is true of us 'older children.' When someone disregards our experience, we feel disregarded. Conversely, when someone regards our experience, we feel regarded.

GOOD INTENTION, BAD APPLICATION

You may read the above scenario and think, "I would never do that!" In reality, most of us frequently do. When someone shares an experience, we often convey that their experience is unimportant, and thus, they are unimportant. Often, we respond in such a way in a misguided attempt to help the other. We often give such responses from a good heart and good intention, usually because we care and don't want the other to struggle. Nevertheless, in reality, we are disregarding their experience; we are wadding up their experience and throwing it in the trash. It's a good intention but a bad application. They are hearing that their experience doesn't make sense and that their experience does not have value. We are communicating that they should not be experiencing what they are experiencing.

The message that ends up being conveyed is, "You're wrong to experience it that way, and you're also dumb to experience it that way." Thus, we've made things worse, despite the good intention. For example:

> *Person 1: Sometimes, I'm afraid to talk to my teacher about certain things.*
> *Person 2: That's silly. There's no reason for you to be afraid of your teacher.*
> *Person 1: I was so disappointed I didn't get to do that with my friend.*
> *Person 2: It just didn't work out. You're fine. Maybe next time.*
> *Person 1: What he said earlier really hurt my feelings.*
> *Person 2: What? He didn't mean anything bad by that.*
> *Person 1: I was so embarrassed by what she did.*
> *Person 2: Don't be embarrassed. It was no big deal.*

This can be even more difficult and volatile if the other's experience personally involves us.

> *Person 1: Sometimes I'm afraid to talk to you about certain things.*
> *Person 2: That's silly. There's no reason for you to be afraid of me.*
> *Person 1: I was so disappointed I didn't get to do that with you.*
> *Person 2: It just didn't work out. You're fine. Maybe next time.*
> *Person 1: What you said earlier really hurt my feelings.*
> *Person 2: What? I didn't mean anything bad by that.*

Person 1: I was so embarrassed by what you did.
Person 2: Don't be embarrassed. It was no big deal.

Again, we often respond in such a way in an attempt to help the other, *and* there is the added component of defending ourselves. But again, the message that ends up being conveyed is, "You're wrong to experience it that way, and you're also *dumb* to experience it that way." Thus, we've made things worse, not better, despite the good intention.

If a child came to you crying because of a skinned knee, you could respond, "There have been billions of skinned knees in the history of the world, and no one has ever died from one. You're fine." You would be totally correct but absolutely wrong. You would be correct in the content, the facts and the information but absolutely wrong in the relationship. Sadly, the primary takeaway for the child would be, "That person doesn't care about me and is not safe. Next time, I'll find someone who cares about me and is safe." Regardless of age, when someone's experience is disregarded, they have the same perspective.

NAKED & FREEZING

An ancient proverb says, "Singing a joyful song to a sorrowful heart is like yanking someone's clothes off of them on a cold winter day!" While this sounds preposterous, most of us unwittingly do this. When someone shares their heartache or struggle, we often respond with:

"Well, it could be worse!"
OR
"At least you're not as bad off as that other person."

OR

"I've had a worse situation than that."

OR

"People's lives are being threatened all around the world, and you're upset about your situation?!"

OR

Something similar.

Such responses disregard the other's experience and, thus disregard the person. This is the same as yanking someone's clothes off of them on a cold winter day.

EAT YOUR BRUSSELS SPROUTS!

Glenn:

I hate (and I use the word hate here) Brussels sprouts. When I was a child, my mother would serve Brussels sprouts and respond to my resistance to eating them with something like, "Eat your Brussels sprouts because there are children starving in India."

Even at a young age, I thought, "Well, ship 'em. It's a win-win. We save the starving children in India, and I don't have to eat Brussels sprouts!" I never said that to my mother (or I wouldn't be here today), but I did not understand her point. I didn't know whether thinking about starving children was supposed to make the Brussels sprouts taste better or worse. Regardless, I did not like Brussels sprouts then, and I still do not like them today. Being aware of another's experience did not change my experience.

POKER, WINE AND KIRKLANDS

Glenn: I love playing Texas Hold 'em poker and may or may not be decent at it.

Phyllis: I don't like poker. I don't dislike poker either. I despise poker.

Glenn: However, you would not know this if you observed our interaction following my latest ridiculous, unfair, painful, conspiratorial exit from a poker tournament. (Some medical evidence suggests I am the unluckiest poker player in the world.) The reality is she doesn't care about poker, but she cares deeply about me. So, she engages with me in my experience and emotion.

Phyllis: Glenn also loves wine, and while I don't despise wine, I have no real interest in it. However, when he tells me about the latest deal he got on a French Bordeaux on Ebay, I engage with him because he is important to me, and I enjoy his experience and his joy.

*Glenn: Neither Phyllis nor I are big shoppers. EXCEPT: Phyllis **loves** shopping at Kirklands, a small home decor retail chain. Each store is usually a few thousand square feet. (As a point of reference, Walmart stores range from about 100,000 to over a quarter of a million square feet.)*

There is a Kirklands near my office. When Phyllis goes there, she will call to see if I can meet her. I love doing that, not because I love Kirklands or shopping, but because I adore her. Going with her is fun, a bit of an impromptu date.

You can walk around an entire Kirklands and see everything in the store in minutes, but the two of us can spend hours talking, reading, laughing, enjoying and then, finally purchasing a few deeply discounted items. Here is a picture of one such item Phyllis especially liked and purchased:

She set it on our bathroom counter, so we could see and enjoy it every day.

Problem: The underline seems misplaced to me. It should be under "love" or "you" and not under "with." Thus, I would read it aloud with an exaggerated emphasis on "with."

After several times of this, Phyllis said, "Babe, I feel sad when you say that. Now when I see it, I hear the way you say it, and it doesn't feel as special."

I realized I had disregarded her experience, thus, disregarding her. I was so bummed that I had messed up the specialness of the saying for her. I had diminished her enjoyment of something that had been *drawing her to me. I was moved never to say it that way again!*

LUKE! LUKE! LUKE! LUKE! LUKE!

Echo:

While watching my son's soccer game, I noticed an enthusiastic mom sitting near us on the sidelines. At one point during the game, her son was knocked down by another player. Instead of jumping right back up, the boy curled into a ball on the field while holding his knee. We watched to see if he was ok, and during these moments of concern, his mom yelled unceasingly, "You're OK, Luke! Luke, you're OK! You're OK, Luke! Luke, LUKE, you're OK Luke." It became almost comical, as though she was stuck on a recorded loop.

As a mom, I related to her intention. Her son was hurt, and she wanted him to be OK. She wanted to encourage and reassure him. I've responded the same way when my children have gotten hurt. But that day, I processed her response through the Connection Codes. All I could think was, "Your intentions are good, but you are disregarding his experience and, therefore, disregarding him. Don't tell him he is OK. He will be OK when he is OK. Tell him you see him and understand his pain. Tell him you can relate. He needs you to regard his experience, so he can process it. Then, he will be OK."

I think all parents do this at times. We so badly want our children to be OK that we try to hurry them out of the pain instead of sitting in the pain with them. We must shift our response so that we regard their experience and, therefore, regard them. That is how we create Identity, safety and connection.

This brings us to one of the bigger Connection Codes puzzle pieces. Although there are several dozen versions of it, because of its significance, it is worthwhile learning to spell it correctly.

(RHYMES WITH SHOE AND GLUE)
(ALWAYS THE CORRECT RESPONSE,
ALWAYS THE RIGHT ANSWER)

Again, there are many versions of Oooo, and you'll figure out what works for your relationships. The Oooo can sound like:

Mmmm

Ahhh

Ohhh

OK

Hmmm

Oh wow

I hear you

Yeah, I get that

Mmm hmm
(or numerous other variations)

AAAAY

Glenn:

We held a Connection Codes workshop in British Columbia, and at this point in the presentation, a man in the front row raised his hand. When I called on him, he said, "Aaaay." I said, "Huh?" He said, "Round here, that's pronounced Aaaay." Responding to my puzzled look, he said, "The Oooo-, round here, it'd be pronounced Aaaay." Through the weekend we noticed this very thing, as in:

Aaaay yeah, that'd be tough.

Aaaay, I get that.

Aaaay, OK, I could see that.

Regardless of how it sounds, the Oooo is designed to convey presence, to help the person sharing to feel heard and seen. This is especially significant as we delve into vulnerable issues.

Note that the Oooo is not agreeing with the other but simply conveying that you hear them and are present with them. Also, research shows that an audible response activates the brain of the person sharing, so audible is important (versus simply nodding or smiling).

Additionally, the Oooo buys you time, time to hear the other's perspective as well as time to consider your own. The Oooo helps you not to attempt to defend, explain, fix, justify, etc., but just be present and hear.

> *Filling the world with Oooos -*
> *one interaction at a time.*

FOLLOW THE ENERGY

When someone says or does something, we can resist their energy or follow their energy. Following someone's energy creates safety, which facilitates connection. *Not* following their energy creates unsafety, which blocks connection.

For example:

> Jane: Ugh, I hate Christmas.
> Shelly: What? You hate Christmas?! Christmas is awesome. I love Christmas! How can you hate Christmas?! You should love Christmas! Why do you feel that way?
> Jane: When I was twelve, my dad left me and my sister and mom a week before Christmas, so it always brings back painful memories for me.
> Shelly: Girl, that was years ago. You gotta let that go. You need to forgive and move on. Besides, you're missing out. Christmas is great!

In this scenario, Shelly is resisting Jane's energy. Jane is conveying something that matters to her; there is energy in it. When Shelly resists Jane's energy, Jane will feel disregarded because her experience is disregarded. She will catalog that it is not safe to be vulnerable with Shelly and will be less likely to share in the future. Their relationship will be hindered, and the depth of their connection will be limited.

OR

Jane: Ugh, I hate Christmas.
Shelly: Oooo, wow, that's intense. What happens for you with that?
Jane: When I was twelve, my dad left me and my sister and mom a week before Christmas, so it always brings back painful memories for me.
Shelly: Oh yeah, that's a lot. That'd be tough.
Jane: Yeah, it is. It's always hard for us.
Shelly: Mmmm, I get that.

In this scenario, Shelly is following Jane's energy. When Shelly follows Jane's energy, Jane will feel regarded because her experience is regarded. She will catalog that it is safe to be vulnerable with Shelly and will be more likely to share in the future. Their relationship will benefit and the depth of their connection will increase. Another example:

Joe: You never listen to me!
Sue: Are you kidding me?! I listen to you all the time.
Joe: Oh please, you do not.
Sue: I absolutely do. That's about all I do when we're together: listen, listen, listen because all you do is talk, talk, talk!!

OR

Joe: You never listen to me!
Sue: Oooo, wow, mmm. What happens with that?
Joe: Well, you're always interrupting me. Like you don't hear me or don't care what I'm saying.

> Sue: Oooo . . .
> Joe: I hate that. It feels like I don't exist when people interrupt me.
> Sue: Oooo, that sounds awful. How can I help with that?

Resisting someone's energy conveys judgement about their perspective and implies that they are wrong and dumb. Following someone's energy helps create safe space for them. Once again, Ooooing is a powerfully effective way to follow someone's energy, convey presence and safety and facilitate connection.

Additionally, in resisting someone's energy, we may be correct regarding content, the facts and figures. We might be able to win a court case and prove to a judge and jury that the other's perspective is inaccurate or incorrect. However, in so doing, we lose connection and damage the relationship. The goal is to win in the relationship not to win the court case.

As we progress in our ability to Oooo, we are able to hear the other on a deeper and deeper level. This allows us to hear what is happening within the other even when we believe they're inaccurate. We then can help the other process the emotions that shut down cognition.

100/50/10

> *Glenn:*
> *A couple was sitting in my office for our third session. She had become activated about an issue between them and turning to her husband stated*

emphatically, "You do that a hundred times a day." I'm pretty good at math, so I calculated and knew she was inaccurate. (100 divided by 16 waking hours a day is about once every ten minutes.) I was certain he could calculate that same math; nonetheless, he Ooooed her.

She said a couple more sentences then said, "It may not be a hundred, but it's like fifty times a day." (Once every twenty minutes? Still no way.) He Ooooed her. She said another sentence or two then said, "I know it's at least ten times a day." (Still unlikely.) He Ooooed her.

She said another sentence, then said "You do this all the time." (I wasn't sure how to calculate that.) He Ooooed her and reached to touch her hand. Then, she said, "I'm not sure how much you actually do this, but it feels like a lot. And it really hurts." He Ooooed her and said, "I get it." Then, he leaned toward her and pulled her toward him.

This was a major turning point in this couple's life. They said in the past such a statement would have led to a conflict lasting for days, weeks or months. After a few minutes, she apologized for her unfair accusation. He laughed gently and said he was glad she said it, because it let him know the extent of what was happening with her. Because he followed her energy by Ooooing her, the interaction did not escalate, and they connected. We call this a Magic Moment!

BUG BITE

5-year-old Grandson (crying as he runs into our house): Papa, I got a bug bite.

Glenn (Papa) (knowing there have been billions of bug bites in the history of human existence, knowing the intensity of the grandson's emotional experience far surpassed the intensity of his pain experience, knowing the grandson would be OK very soon, etc.): Oooo youch! Where did you get a bug bite?

Grandson (crying stopping instantly, replaced by studious look): From a bug. (pausing, seemingly concerned about his grandfather's intellectual capability) Papa, that's why it's called a bug bite.

Papa: Oh right. So where on your body did you get a bug bite?

Grandson (yelling as he runs back outside to play): On my arm. It's OK now.

WHY? VS WHAT HAPPENS?

In relational interactions, we don't ask "Why?" about behavior. People typically don't know why they say and do things, and even if they figure it out, it rarely helps connection. Instead, we ask "What happens?" (or "What happened?" or "What's happening?") "Why?" comes across as an accusation; "What happens?" is an invitation. "Why?" indicts; "What happens?" invites.

"What happens?" is an extension of the Oooo, the second phrase. "What happens?" invites the other into their own experience. This conveys safety and lets them know we will be there for them. They then can explore what *is* happening within them, which can lead to discovering things they previously had not realized. This further promotes partnering and connection. For example:

> *Brooke: I'm nervous about going into labor and my baby's birth.*
> *Erica: Oh, girl, why are you nervous?*
> *Brooke: I've been thinking about stuff that could go wrong.*
> *Erica: Oh, don't think that way. This is your third baby; you'll be fine. You did great with your first two. Besides, there have been billions of births before, so you have nothing to be nervous about. Just stop thinking like that!*

OR

> *Brooke: I'm nervous about going into labor and my baby's birth.*
> *Erica: Oooo, what happens for you with that?*
> *Brooke: I've been thinking about stuff that could go wrong.*
> *Erica: Oh yeah, that can be intense. What's the toughest part for you?*
> *Brooke: (Shares what she fears.)*
> *Erica: Mmmm, that's a lot. I see how that'd be hard for you.*
> *Brooke: Yeah.*

Echo:

When we ask our children "Why?" they did something, we are asking them to analyze their behavior, which is a pretty advanced skill even for adults. When confronted with this question, many kids (and adults) shut down and get defensive. When we ask, "What happens?" we provide an invitation for communication and understanding. By attempting to understand their perspective, the frustration we feel about their behavior often diminishes.

We have found the more we partner with our kids, the more peaceful and productive we are as a family. One of the ways we do this is by slowing down our reaction to unmet expectations. The "what happens" is a great way to do this.

One of our kids has a difficult time staying focused and following through on tasks. It is easy to get frustrated and criticize this tendency, but that just escalates the interaction, derailing the task further and causing disconnect between us and the child. We have found the more effective response is to ask what's happening when they don't follow through. We then partner to find solutions that will help them follow through. When we are intentional about this, the task gets completed, and we stay connected.

I MISSED IT

The third phrase to add to the Oooo and What happens is "I missed it." This helps convey your desire to be present for the other and connect with them. All of us miss things with others for a variety of reasons. Sometimes, it is because the other person did not convey things clearly. Sometimes, it is because we were not paying attention. Sometimes, it is a simple misunderstanding of meaning. Regardless of the cause, conveying that you missed it helps to keep the interaction from escalating. For example:

Larry: You didn't do that the way I wanted you to.

John: I did it the way you said. You just didn't explain it adequately. You needed to make it more clear!

OR

Larry: You didn't do that the way I wanted you to.

John: Oooo, wow, I missed that. Can you help me understand better?

Also, conveying that you missed something and need help invites the other to partner with you in a common quest. Accusing or indicting them for their part in you misunderstanding separates or unpartners you.

> *Go to Amazon.com and order an extra large box of Oooos. While you're there, get a smaller box of "What happens?" and a little box of "I missed it."*

STILL FACE

In the 1970s, Dr Ed Tronick did a series of experiments called the still face experiments. The original experiment consisted of a baby and mom sitting together. There was no food, drink, toy, etc. involved; there was simply "presence." At a given moment, the mom would change her facial expression to totally blank, what Dr Tronick called a still face. Thus, the mom would be physically there but not relationally there. Nothing else would change. There was no yelling, pinching, etc.; there simply was a still face.

The baby would notice immediately and become agitated. The baby's response would escalate to the point of a loss of composure and posture: wiggling, crying, squealing, screaming, kicking, etc. At a given moment, the mom would reengage, and the baby's uneasiness would deescalate quickly.

Numerous variations of this experiment have been conducted with the baby's dad or another caregiver with consistently similar results. The baby would escalate in response to a still face then deescalate when the adult reengaged. In one variation, the adult would leave the room, and the baby would be fine, often for several minutes. The adult leaving the room was actually *better* for the baby than the adult being physically present but relationally absent.

In another variation, four total strangers stood in front of a baby. The baby did not know any of them, and none of them knew the baby. Three of the adults were instructed to give a still face; the fourth was instructed to be 'present' with the baby. There was no food, drink, toy, etc.; there was simply 'presence.' The baby would begin honing in on the non-still face person and give less and less attention to the three still face people. Eventually, the still face people seemed to no longer exist in the baby's world. The baby would not do this intentionally; this was not a cognizant effort. The baby was not contemplating who would be of the most benefit in the future. The baby was coded to move toward relational presence and away from relational absence.

Watching these experiments, it is easy to think, "That's a baby experience," but that's not a baby experience; that's a human experience. Adults experience the same thing when presented with a still face; we all are just older babies! As adults, we are expected not to cry, squeal, scream, kick and throw things, though many adults do. Receiving a still face is just as unbearable for adults.

CONSIDER

You have been invited to a friend's house for dinner. You arrive and ring the doorbell. Your friend opens the door and, instead of giving a greeting, blankly stares at you. You and your friend walk into the kitchen, but as you talk, your friend only stares at you.

What if nothing you did or said elicited a response from your friend? How long would it be before this became awkward? How long would it be before it became unbearable? How long would it take for your mind to race and your blood pressure to rise and the discomfort of enduring their absence of response cause you to want to leave? How long would it take for you to actually leave? How long would it take for you to call for help?

OR

You have been invited to a friend's house for dinner. You arrive and ring the doorbell. Your friend opens the door and greets you with a smile and an embrace then moves to the side and gestures for you to enter the house. You and your friend walk into the kitchen, and your friend asks how your week has been.

Your friend nods as you speak, asks follow up questions, laughs when you tell a funny story and empathizes when you share about a challenging moment you had that day. Then, your friend shares about how their own week has been.

How would this experience compare to the first scenario? In the first scenario, your friend has presented a still face. Humans can receive a still face for only a few seconds before becoming uncomfortable and having a strong urge to change it. Also, people can be unaware of giving a still face and rarely is it with bad intention.

Glenn:
For many years, Phyllis owned a sizable business and because she was the owner, she handled business from the first communication of the day (sometimes as early as 5:00 am) until the last one (sometimes midnight or later). While she was not actually working that entire time, she had to be available to handle problems immediately and quickly.

In such a scenario, if I entered the room and greeted her and she didn't respond, I felt as though I was falling; it was a visceral experience for me. It didn't matter that Phyllis was being a responsible CEO, and it didn't matter that I knew that. It didn't matter that we had a great relationship, or that she would respond to me momentarily. It didn't matter that this is my field of study and that I knew what was happening. In that moment, I felt like I was falling because my greeting did not receive a response; I received a still face.

This was not an indictment of Phyllis; she was doing the good and right thing. This had nothing to do with Phyllis, even though it was all about Phyllis. This was simply what happened inside of me. I was not trying to experience a still face; I simply did. It was important that my response to her was not unkind, but the still face experience is nonetheless difficult. That is the human condition.

Echo:
When I am speaking to an audience, I find my eyes continually drawn to the individuals who look engaged. When I first begin speaking, my eyes travel over the room, but as the minutes pass I find my attention focuses on the people who nod or smile, whose facial expression and body language indicate a responsiveness to what I am saying. The Connection Codes helped me realize I am drawn to the responsive audience member because of my coding to move away from a still face and move towards a non-still face.

The Connection Codes have also helped me to be aware of when I am giving a still face. At times I give a still face because I am exhausted or distracted, but usually I give a still face when I am flooded with emotion and struggling to engage. In those moments, it helps to have someone who knows the Connection Codes to ask me what is happening. This helps me process my emotion and reconnect.

This has been a significant tool in my marriage. Now when my husband notices my still face, he asks me what is happening. This creates awareness between us that has reduced our times of disconnect from days/weeks to minutes/seconds, transforming our marriage and life.

THE WORST MARRIAGE THERAPIST IN TENNESSEE

Glenn:

A client burst into my office, flopped on the couch, pointed his finger at me and declared "You're the worst marriage therapist in Tennessee!"

I personally know two marriage therapists in Tennessee who are worse than me, so I knew he was wrong. I was certain I could stand before a judge and easily win a court case showing I am not the worst marriage therapist in Tennessee. I had no idea why he was making such a defamatory, inaccurate declaration. Nonetheless, I managed to respond, "Oooo, wow, that sounds like a lot. What's happening with that?"

I had seen him and his wife for the first time the previous week. At the conclusion of that session, we had scheduled our next session for the same time the next week, the session that now began with his declaration. He had emailed about an hour and a half after our first session to confirm our second session. I had managed to respond to that email with a "Yes."

He emailed four more times to reconfirm the appointment. I could see the subject line and the first sentence, so I knew I had already addressed the issue. I did not manage to respond to those emails. Problem: What had he received from me with the second, third, fourth and fifth emails? A STILL FACE- an unbearable human experience!

He recapped the information concerning the emails, particularly the ones that went unanswered. As he conveyed this, I saw the fear and pain in his eyes and heard it in his voice. He was counting on me to help save his marriage, to save his family (they have three young children) and, yes, to save his life. He was depending on me to help salvage a dire situation with endless ramifications, and I gave him a still face. He clearly and repeatedly received a message of: "I do not care. You, your situation, your pain mean nothing to me. You have no value to me, so little in fact, that I will not even respond to you." He was certain he would arrive at my office, and the door would be locked. I would not be there, and he would be doomed.

As his tirade progressed, I continued to Oooo him. He began to calm and ended up apologizing *profusely. The entire interaction took two to three minutes.*

He had come directly from work and arrived before his wife. When she arrived, he conveyed to her what had transpired. I was concerned about her reaction, as she easily could have responded with, "You said WHAT?!?! Are you crazy?! Are you trying to get him not *to help us?!*

Instead, she did the very thing we had covered the week before: she Ooooed him! She even reached to touch his arm as she continued, "Aw Babe, that's so much. I didn't know you were experiencing that all week; that's awful." Although tears did not drop from his eyes, they did form, and there were plenty from mine. And, just so you know, they're doing great now, marvelously connected.

The success of that interchange and their subsequent success stemmed from an Oooo. I knew I had to slow down the interaction, so I simply Ooooed him. Also, Ooooing him bought me some time. I did not know why he declared that I'm the worst marriage therapist in the state, but I knew me Ooooing him would give me time and give him safe space.

By the time he completed his tirade, I understood his perspective. If the very person to whom he is turning and entrusting the future success of his marriage, family and life is not even going to show up and doesn't even care, then yes, that is the worst marriage therapist in Tennessee!

> **STILL FACE IN ACTION**
> *Her (exasperated): Are you even listening to me?!*
> *Him (puzzled, thinking to himself): That's a strange way to begin a conversation.*

MOVE TOWARD KINDNESS

We are coded to move toward kindness; we are coded to move away from unkindness. As much as possible, it is beneficial to be with people who are kind to us.

This coding can create a difficult struggle when involving those with whom we are biologically related; we are coded to connect with the members of our family of origin. However, if they are unkind to us, that coding is now at odds with the coding to move away from unkindness. Many such relationships continue, not because one or both experience the relationship positively, but because they share a family tree. This produces a painful, tension-filled scenario. If a stranger treated us as some family members do, we would never consider interacting with that person again.

The same can be true of ongoing relationships, such as a boss, coworker, teacher, classmate, neighbor, etc. Life can become a daily struggle when circumstances require being with people from whom we experience unkindness. Some studies report people will take up to a 38% decrease in pay in order to be in a work environment where they are treated with kindness and feel valued. Even when financial loss is incurred, individuals will choose to move toward kindness.

Phyllis:
Some years ago, I asked Glenn, "Babe, why do

you pursue relationships with people who don't want a relationship with you?"

He seemed befuddled by the question and replied, "Cause that's what we're supposed to do; that's what a good person does!"

I replied, "No, it's not." He reacted as though my perspective was blasphemous, but now he says it changed his life!

Sometime later our adult children addressed the same issue with us:

"Dad, you expend your time and energy on people who don't like you and who never will. You devote yourself to people who are unkind to you, so you have nothing left for those who want to be your friend."

This was revolutionary! Now Glenn spends his time and energy with people who are kind to him and wow, what a difference!

An important caveat: this does not mean we do not do acts of service, whether for kind or unkind people. We certainly should, even if we do not receive Identity or kindness. Nonetheless, we are not coded to live life with those from whom we do not receive Identity or kindness. Situations that involve people who are unkind to us deplete and defeat us. Connecting with those from whom we receive Identity energizes and empowers us!

WE MUST *FEEL* HEARD

In the mid-20th century, a natural disaster led to a large influx of young children in an orphanage. The workers in the orphanage were vastly outnumbered by the children and struggled attempting to keep up with the babies' basic needs. A psychologist went to observe and record what was happening.

The caregivers did their best to maintain the basics but were always behind. In his journal, the psychologist described the chaotic environment and the continuous sound of babies' crying, including throughout the night. After some time, he notated that the babies were adjusting to their new environment. There was not as much crying and at times there were periods of quiet.

He had been sitting out of the way against a wall, and as the situation stabilized, he moved his chair closer for better observation. In his notes, he then wrote: "They didn't adjust; they gave up!" He then wrote, "The babies are no longer here." He elaborated that the babies' facial expressions were blank. He would look in their eyes, and they would not respond. The babies had called out for help endlessly but did not receive the response they craved and needed and eventually gave up.

We must *feel* heard. If not, we get louder and louder, but eventually give up. This is as true for adults as it is for children. If we do not *feel* heard, we receive the message that we do not have value, and we lose Identity.

Notice the emphasis is on *feeling* heard, not on being heard. This is not about the anatomy of the ear, whether or not it is functioning. Being heard and feeling heard are two distinctly different things! Recognizing this distinction can bring a significant difference in connection. Telling someone you heard them by declaring "I heard you!" does not satisfy their need to *feel* heard. And, if someone does not *feel* heard, they will get louder and louder until they either feel heard or they give up. When someone *feels* heard, they receive Identity, they experience safety and they can connect.

Echo:
We must feel heard. This concept has given me a different lens for how I see my children's behavior. The cultural narrative seems to be that kids fuss and fight because they are immature, selfish and undisciplined. I believed that for many years, and it created a lot of impatience and quick judgement in how I responded to them. This changed as my perspective changed, and I slowed down to observe my children more.

I also began noticing other children and was astounded by what I observed. I would see a marked change if they did not feel heard and regarded, whether by another child, a parent or someone else. This frequently would lead to them getting louder and louder, sometimes with yelling and hitting involved, in an effort to be heard.

Observing this led me to change the way I parent. Now when my kids have a conflict or when their emotions escalate, I slow down, ask questions and listen to their perspective. This approach has changed the atmosphere in our home and brought so much communication and peace.

ATTACHMENT THEORY

Most of the Connection Codes fit under the umbrella of Attachment Theory, a set of principles regarding how people attach with others in relationships. The term "attachment theory" was coined by Ursula Bowlby in discussions with her husband, Dr John Bowlby. Legend has it that John liked the term "love theory," but Ursula thought that sounded strange. We don't especially like the term "attachment" either, as it sounds somewhat clinical.

There have been countless contributors to the massive amount of research conducted concerning Attachment Theory. However, Attachment Theory can be boiled down to two questions:

Will you be there for me?

AND

Am I good enough for you?

If two people both can answer yes to both questions, they can attach, connect, have a relationship. Bear in mind, *both* parties must answer yes to *both* questions. If either party does not answer with a clear yes to both questions, the relationship will be hindered.

Phyllis:

Suppose we meet, and you ask, "Will you be there for me?" If I respond, "Yeah, sure, probably," how confident will you feel moving forward with our relationship? Will you trust me?

Or suppose you ask, "Am I good enough for you?"

and I respond, "I guess so. I mean, I've seen worse. So yeah sure, you're fine." How comfortable will you feel pursuing a relationship with me? You are coded to need an emphatic Yes in order to connect with me. And it must be a clear yes. My responses did not include a "No," but they did not include the mandatory "Yes."

Perhaps you believe I will be there for you, but you do not think you are good enough for me. In that case, you know I am reliable, but you do not feel safe to be authentic with me. You do not believe I view you positively, so you do not feel adequate to actually be my friend or at least that I want you as my friend.

Or perhaps you believe you are good enough for me, but you do not believe I will be there for you. In this case, you cannot rely on me. You do not feel confident that I will be available when you need me. We cannot have a relationship because you cannot trust me.

When both of us are able to answer yes to both questions, trust and security are established. Connection then can grow out of that foundation.

MY DEAR FRIEND BEYONCÉ

Glenn:

A friend gave us tickets for second row seats to a Beyoncé concert in Nashville. At one point during the concert, Beyoncé looked at me and said, "I love you, Nashville!" Surmising that Nashville was her chosen nickname for me, I was delighted to learn she felt that way and jumped onstage to be with my new friend. Clearly, she was there for me, and she conveyed that I was good enough for her.

Much to my surprise, disappointment and pain, her security team did not believe in Attachment Theory and quickly made that clear. (Apparently, they need therapy.) OK, I made up the second part, but she really did look at me (along with several thousand other people) and say, "I love you." Nonetheless, we do not have a relationship, as Queen B is not there for me, and she, or at least her security team, does not think I am good enough for her.

If I followed her home to pursue this new friendship, I would be labeled a stalker. Beyoncé's 'being there for me' was influenced by the several hundred dollar price tag on the tickets.*

If you are there for me (as Beyoncé was), but it becomes clear that I am not good enough for you, then I view you as a celebrity. If I am convinced I am good enough for you, but you are not there for me, then I cannot trust you and will not consider you a friend.

*I do not wish to disparage Beyoncé or her team- I trust they're all delightful people.

CODED FOR EMPATHY

Humans are coded to experience what those around them are experiencing. In research conducted by Dr Paul Ekman, participants were shown a series of pictures of people's faces. While viewing the pictures, they would begin mimicking the facial expressions of the people shown in the pictures. When the picture showed a person crying, the participant's face began showing sadness. When the picture showed a person laughing, the participant's face began showing joy. The participants did not know the people in the pictures or what prompted the facial expressions. Nonetheless, they automatically experienced the emotion of the other. We are coded for empathy, which leads us to connect.

Research suggests that we have mirror neurons in the brain. Some evidence indicates that we can experience a particular sensation when observing another doing an action as if we ourselves are doing that action. This further underscores the empathic aspect of human experience.

VULNERABILITY ↔ SAFETY

Imagine you are exiting a building, and there is a set of stairs. You see that someone has fallen down the stairs and is lying on the ground bleeding. You are *coded* to respond to that person; you are hard-wired to want to help. You do not ask their Zodiac sign, political party affiliation, religious background or nation of origin. They are in a position of vulnerability, and you are coded to respond to them by providing safety, to give assistance.

This reaction is automatic; you do not have to contemplate the situation. Moreover, you would not turn to a friend and say, "Wow, that's a lot of blood. I bet that hurt; wonder if he's still alive. Oh well, where d'ya wanna go to lunch?" There is a pressing internal urge to help the hurting, an innate desire to assist someone in a position of vulnerability.

UNLESS

Last month you were in a similar situation, but when you rushed over to help, the "injured" person rolled over, pulled out a gun and robbed you. You discovered it was fake blood and a setup. The person was not actually in a position of vulnerability, but in a position of attack. Because of *that* experience, you are now not certain *this* injured person is in a position of vulnerability, so your brain signals you to be cautious and *not* help. There is now an extra ingredient in the scenario, which alters your normal coding response. You are coded to want to help, but the extra ingredient reprograms you and interferes with your coding. Thus your "reprogramming" is at odds with your coding.

AND

They are coded to *accept* your help; they are hard-wired to *want* your help. They do not ask your Zodiac sign, political party affiliation, religious background or nation of origin. You are in a position of safety and offering assistance, and they are coded to respond in their vulnerability to accept assistance.

This reaction is automatic; they do not have to contemplate the situation.

UNLESS

Last month they were in a similar situation, but when someone rushed over to 'help,' the 'helper' pulled a gun and robbed them. The 'helper' was taking advantage of the injured person's vulnerability. The 'helper' was not in a position of safety, but a position of attack. Because of *that* experience, the injured person is not certain you are in a position of safety, so their brain signals them to be cautious and perhaps *not* accept help. There is now an extra ingredient in the scenario, which alters their normal coding response. They are coded to accept help, but the extra ingredient reprograms them and interferes with their coding. Thus, their reprogramming is at odds with their coding.

ALSO

The injured person may counterattack to protect themselves. They may pull away from you and yell, "Get away from me!" Now *your* coding is to move away from *them*, because they are not in a position of vulnerability but in a position of attack.

Connection occurs when a position of vulnerability speaks into a position of safety. However, people hesitate to be vulnerable until they know the other is safe & secure, but they won't know the other is safe & secure until they are vulnerable. This impasse requires someone taking a risk.

In long term relationships, there are extra ingredients that alter the coded response of one or both people. There may be hesitancy for vulnerability because of unsuccessful interactions from the past. Or there may be hesitancy to *believe* the other actually *is* being vulnerable because of unsuccessful interactions from the past. Nevertheless, if one continues to be in a position of vulnerability, the other will respond with safety. And if one continues to offer safety, the other eventually will respond with vulnerability. Vulnerability invites safety; safety invites vulnerability.

> *I don't want to be vulnerable until I know you're safe, but I won't know you're safe until I'm vulnerable. Also, I don't offer safety until you're vulnerable, but you won't want to be vulnerable until you know I'm safe. So, someone has to take a risk.*

SECTION 1 TAKEAWAYS

Identity is the #1, fundamental, foundational, most pressing human need, more important than food, water or oxygen.

If you disregard a person's experience, you disregard the person. Conversely, if you regard a person's experience, you regard the person.

A good intention can have a bad application.

The 3 phrases:
    Oooo is always the correct response.
    Why vs What happens.
    Add I missed it.

Follow the energy; don't resist the energy.

We are coded to move toward kindness and away from unkindness.

We must *feel* heard; if not, we get louder but eventually give up.

Attachment theory=2 questions: Will you be there for me? Am I good enough for you? We both must receive yes answers to both questions to connect.

Connection occurs when a position of vulnerability speaks into a position of safety. Vulnerability invites safety; safety invites vulnerability.

Following is the Identity Experience Assignment. Be sure to take the time to do the Experience Assignments, because the power of the Connection Codes is not in the content but in the experience.

While the Experience Assignments are often done with family members, they can be done with friends, coworkers or even total strangers. There can be great power in doing them in any setting or relationship.

IDENTITY EXPERIENCE ASSIGNMENT

I receive identity when

I lose identity when

I receive identity from *you* when

I lose identity with *you* when

I give *you* a still face when

I receive a still face from *you* when

IDENTITY EXPERIENCE EXAMPLE 1

I receive identity when I make a good grade on an exam.

I lose identity when my classmate makes fun of my handwriting.

I receive identity from you when you listen to me describe the project I am working on.

I lose identity with you when you answer the phone while I'm talking about my project.

I give you a still face when you talk about your family being amazing. I don't think they like me, so I don't know what to say.

I receive a still face from you when I say something critical about your parents.

IDENTITY EXPERIENCE EXAMPLE 2

I receive identity when my children thank me for making dinner.

I lose identity when you criticize me for the mess I made while making dinner.

I receive identity from you when you tell me I am a good mama.

I lose identity with you when you come home and comment on our messy house before greeting me or the children.

I give you a still face when I feel a rush of emotion about something you said, but I don't know how to respond.

I receive a still face from you when you don't acknowledge that you've heard me.

IDENTITY EXPERIENCE EXAMPLE 3

I receive identity when my editor publishes my article.

I lose identity when my article is not chosen for publication.

I receive identity from you when you tell me you are proud of me for getting published.

I lose identity with you when you forget to read my article.

I give you a still face when you criticize my writing while praising another writer's work.

I receive a still face when I write you a letter, and you don't acknowledge it.

IDENTITY EXPERIENCE EXAMPLE 4

I receive identity when co-workers defer to me and my ideas.

I lose identity when my dad criticizes my career path.

I receive identity from you when you talk about how good of a dad I am and how close to me our kids feel.

I lose identity with you when you criticize me for being preoccupied with work, especially when I feel like I'm trying my best to provide for our family.

I give you a still face when you ask about our finances.

I receive a still face when I ask you about a recent purchase.

Section 1
Focus

Be aware of Identity this week.

Notice when you gain or lose Identity, and tell someone you trust about it.

Also, notice when those around you gain or lose Identity.

Notice how you affect the Identity of others.

Make it your goal to give Identity to each person with whom you interact.

SECTION 2

Emotion: A Human Right

All humans require oxygen; there are no exceptions. If someone says, "I don't use oxygen anymore; I matured past it; I've transcended the need for it," do not believe them. Regardless of their insistence, know that this is simply untrue. Oxygen is part of human existence and experience. It is mandatory and a fundamental human right. Limiting the proper processing of oxygen has terrible effect and results in incalculable damage. The absence of oxygen is catastrophic for the human condition.

All humans require blood; there are no exceptions. If someone says, "I don't use blood anymore; I matured past it; I've transcended the need for it," do not believe them. Regardless of their insistence, know that this is simply untrue. Blood is part of human existence and experience. It is mandatory and a fundamental human right. Limiting the proper processing of blood has terrible effect and results in incalculable damage. The absence of blood is catastrophic for the human condition.

All humans require emotion; there are no exceptions. If someone says, "I don't do emotion anymore; I matured past it; I've transcended the need for it," do not believe them. Regardless of their insistence, know that this is simply untrue. Emotion is part of human existence and experience. It is mandatory and a fundamental human right. Limiting the proper processing of emotion has terrible effect and results in incalculable damage. The absence of emotion is catastrophic for the human condition.

All humans experience emotion; we are hardwired this way. Emotion is an aspect of the functioning of the brain, just as oxygen is an aspect of the functioning of the lungs and blood is an aspect of the functioning of the heart. This is true of every human everywhere; there are no exceptions. As with oxygen and blood, emotion is not good or bad; it simply is. As with oxygen and blood, there need not be a value judgement; it simply is a mandatory part of the human experience. We do not try to experience emotion; it is automatic and simply what is happening in the brain.

EMOTION AND THE BRAIN

There are five areas in the brain associated with emotion, that 'house' emotion: pleasure, anger, disgust, fear and pain. This is true for every human. While there are countless human emotions, all of them stem from these five regions, with innumerable hybrids and combinations.

The emotion of two of the regions present distinctly enough to identify them separately. Thus research indicates humans experience eight core emotions:

Joy (pleasure)
Anger
Guilt (disgust about an action)
Shame (disgust about oneself)
Fear
Hurt (sharp pain)
Sadness (sustained permeating pain)
Loneliness (chronic pain)

A few ♪s about emotion before we expound upon the eight core emotions.

♪ EMOTION SERVES A PURPOSE

Every human has needs and is born with the capability to convey those needs. Our brains process messages received through our senses. The awareness of these needs originates with emotion. The emotion serves a purpose; it conveys a message to protect and help us. Emotion is not bad; it should not be ignored but honored. It is a guide that attempts to get our attention. As we grow older, this does not change.

Problem: Most of us have received the message that emotion is bad, wrong and a sign of weakness. Through various ways, verbal and nonverbal messages, interactions, situations, circumstances, culture, etc., we have been reprogrammed and learned to resist, shrug off, ignore, suppress, step over, etc. and definitely not share emotion.

If you walk into someone's kitchen and their hand is resting on a hot stove, you would be concerned. Your immediate concern would be about their smoldering flesh, but your bigger concern would be about their lack of reaction–the fact that they were not bothered by the effect of the hot stove and the pain. Their pain is not accomplishing its purpose.

In the same way that physical pain is meant to accomplish something, emotion is meant to accomplish something. Each core emotion sends a message, signaling us to be aware.

> *Summer (Connection Coder and Phyllis & Glenn's youngest daughter):*
> *When I was completing my doctoral program, I was required to do a forty-five minute presentation. Problem: Unlike my parents, I hate public speaking and felt significant levels of fear. I processed the fear numerous times with my family and friends and discussed the message fear was sending: "Danger! Beware! There is a risk, a potential problem."*
>
> *I did not have the option of whether or not to do the presentation, so the conclusion was to be prepared. Fear was telling me to make certain I did not stand in front of a crowd unprepared. I paid attention to the message, was prepared and did well. I am now a doctor and able to pursue my goals!*
>
> **NO FEAR!**
> *Glenn:*
> *(With a thick Australian accent) "That thing can rip your face off Mate! It's a wild animal, ya know!"*

Phyllis and I were at Cape Hillsborough in Australia to see the crowd of kangaroos and wallabies gathered for their daily predawn seaweed feeding fest. They were obviously accustomed to human contact, acting comfortable, friendly and even bold. I interpreted this as a sign to replicate their demeanor and was thoroughly enjoying the beautiful creatures, feeding them seaweed and petting them as I posed for pictures and videos.

At that point, the local ranger approached to cue me into the potential danger. He pointed out the six inch claws on their hind feet and the razor sharp claws on their front feet. He shared about injuries, mild and severe, sustained by excited and oblivious people (like me) encountering these intriguing creatures.

I felt no fear and lots of joy with a behavior that had potential for great harm. My ignorance and lack of awareness facilitated my lack of fear, setting up the possibility for damage. Being fear free could have led to my demise.

Emotion serves a purpose.

♪ EMOTION CONNECTS

Emotion is a universal language. Every human is coded to speak it; every human is coded to understand it. If someone says they feel fear, we understand what they mean because we all know how that emotion feels. All humans have the same emotional coding;

we all experience the same core emotions. Because of this, we can relate to each other.

Unfortunately, most of us have been conditioned *not* to speak our native language of emotion, thus it may take effort to *re*learn. Nonetheless, we are all coded to communicate through the language of emotion.

If you are reading this book, you have the capability to learn a new language. But how long would it take you to become fluent in that language? A year, two years or longer? If you had to learn this new language before you could connect deeply in relationship, it would be a daunting task. Fortunately, the language of emotion is not new for you; it is your original language that simply needs to be reactivated.

As mentioned previously, humans are the least likely species to survive independently and the most likely to thrive interdependently. We are safer, better and stronger when we live connected with others in teamship. Emotion is the language of connection, thus emotion further protects us by facilitating this teamship.

Humans do *not* connect through logistics. Logistics are the facts and figures, the information, the content. Logistics are real and valid, but they do not connect us relationally. Logistics bring us together geographically; emotions bring us together relationally.

If you love mushrooms and you attend the International Mushroom Lovers Convention, you will not connect relationally with another person simply because of your mutual affinity for mushrooms. Liking mushrooms brought you to the same location, but that is *not* what will connect you relationally. You have geographic closeness but not relational closeness. If you meet someone at such a convention and they give you a still face, treat you with unkindness or disregard, resist your energy or in some other way are not present and safe, you will lose Identity and not connect with them, regardless of how much you both love mushrooms.

♪ COMMUNICATE EMOTION, NOT THROUGH EMOTION

It is important to communicate the core emotion, not *through* the emotion. Often someone will say they convey emotion clearly, but usually they are communicating *through* the emotion. For example:

> *Tracy: You're such a jerk; I get sick of how you treat me!*

That is communicating *through* the emotion.

> *Tracy: I feel hurt by what you said; that was really painful for me.*

That is communicating the core emotion.

We connect with each other when we share core emotions, the deeper the emotion, the deeper the connection. Shared emotion pulls people together, bringing connection; unshared emotion pushes people apart, bringing disconnection.

THE LOST GOLDMINE
CONSIDER

If you buy a piece of property and discover gold in the ground, how much is that gold worth?
(Dramatic pause)
Nothing. In and of itself, the gold is worth

nothing. The gold only has value if it is used in transactions.

Additionally, unmined gold actually makes the ground unusable for growing or building. Thus, the gold is a detriment when it is not utilized.

Emotion is the great lost goldmine of relational connection. However, in and of itself, emotion is worth nothing. In relationships, emotion only has value if it is used in transactions.

Additionally, unmined emotion actually makes a relationship unusable for growing or building. Thus, the emotion is a detriment when it is not utilized.

> *Every emotion is an opportunity to connect ... or not.*

A CUP OF TEA

Glenn: For many years in our early marriage, I would ask Phyllis, "Do you want a cup of tea?" More often than not, she would respond with something like, "No thanks. I'm really busy, and I'm too hot to enjoy hot tea right now." I would then feel rejected and carry that wound for a while. Later, she might ask me to do something for her, and I would respond negatively and unkindly.

Problem: The question was a lie, a misrepresentation of the truth. The question itself was based on a false premise; I wasn't really wanting to know if she wanted a cup of tea. The truth was that I was feeling lonely; I was missing her and wanted time with her.

Phyllis: I was clueless what was happening with my partner. And the times we did have tea together, I noticed the mugs getting bigger and the water getting hotter. This would require me to spend more time with him.

Glenn: Now, I realize she was answering the question I asked her, but I was not conveying what was happening with me. I also was clueless.

NO OFFENSE

Glenn:

After several sessions, a couple was connecting beautifully. One day:

Husband: No offense Doc, but what you do is simple. It's really just common sense!

Glenn: Oooo, OK . . . and . . . ?

Husband: Well, I just need to let her know what's really happening with me.

Wife (dramatically and with a huge smile): Yeeeeeuuss!

Yes indeed; they're winning!

♪ EMOTION HAPPENS

Emotion happens to us. We do not choose our emotions. No one awakens in the morning and plans their emotional day. No one says, "Today, I'm going to experience loneliness, fear, shame and joy." If there is an explosion nearby, we instantly feel fear. We do not decide whether or not to feel that emotion. When we lose a loved one, we feel sadness. We do not decide whether or not to feel that emotion.

Emotion happens to us, we cannot control our emotion. We are not responsible for our emotion. We *are* responsible for our next *action*. We are not allowed to key someone's car because we felt hurt by what they said or did. We can't drive 120 mph on the highway and say, "But Officer, I was feeling anger."

This is worth reiterating, as it can be a huge paradigm shift. Emotion happens to us. We are *not* responsible for our emotion. We *are* responsible for our next action.

Telling someone to stop feeling a particular emotion is actually detrimental. They are not trying to feel a particular emotion, so telling them to stop feeling it is counterproductive and doesn't work. You will simply convince them to stop sharing vulnerably with you.

When we are not present with someone sharing, we disregard their experience and they do not *feel* heard. They lose Identity (the #1, fundamental, foundational, most pressing human need) and want to move away, whether geographically or relationally.

When we are simply present with someone sharing, we regard their experience and they *feel* heard. They receive Identity (the #1, fundamental, foundational, most pressing human need) and want to move closer, whether geographically or relationally.

The next time someone says you should not experience a particular emotion, let them know you are not trying to experience that emotion, you simply are. Also, ask them what they would like you to do with that emotion.

We often help people do this in sessions. An example:

> *Rick: I feel hurt when you criticize the movies I like.*
> *Judy: What? No, don't feel hurt. I'm just telling you my opinion. You shouldn't feel hurt about that.*
> *Therapist: Do you think Rick is trying to feel hurt?*
> *Judy: I guess not, but he shouldn't feel hurt about it.*
> *Therapist: Well, the emotion is happening to him. He's not choosing that emotion.*
> *Judy: Oh yeah, right, OK.*
> *Therapist: What would you like him to do when he feels hurt?*
> *Judy: Tell me!*
> *Therapist: So that you can then tell him not to feel hurt and that he shouldn't feel hurt?*
> *Judy: Oh wow, yeah, I guess that doesn't help. I guess that's what you mean by 'disregarding someone's experience, so you're disregarding the person.'*
> *Therapist: Exactly.*
> *Judy: And I guess then he wouldn't want to tell me next time.*
> *Therapist: Can you ask him?*
> *Judy: Ask him what?*
> *Therapist: Ask him if it helps him turn to you more readily when you tell him not to feel an emotion and that he shouldn't feel that emotion.*

Judy (turning to her partner): Um, does it help you turn to me when I tell you not to feel what you're feeling and that you shouldn't feel it?

Rick (smiling, but looking sheepish): Not at all. Most of the time I just stuff it, cause I figure you'll tell me that.

Judy (looking somber): Wow, how often does that happen?

Rick: I feel silly saying it but a lot, probably most days.

Judy: That stinks. So I definitely just need to hear you from now on, just Oooo you, and let you experience what you experience.

Rick (smiling and reaching to hold his partner's hand): Oh my gosh, that would be amazing.

Echo:
I spent many years paralyzed by my emotions. My emotions defined me. I believed they were one of my greatest character flaws. I believed if I just tried harder, if I were a stronger, better, wiser, more grateful person then I would not experience loneliness, fear, sadness and shame so deeply and so often. Believing my emotions were a character flaw lead to me hurting myself and others.

Learning that emotions happen to us has given so much relief to my conscience that I now find myself with the energy needed to process the emotions and choose my next action wisely.

> *Margaret (Connection Coder):*
> *I wish my mom had known the Connection Codes when I was young. I wish she had understood that emotion happens to us, that I wasn't trying to feel joy when I would giggle during church service. I remember once in church I was flooded with joy, and I got in a lot of trouble. The preacher was teaching about Samson and the story of the Philistines from Judges 15. He talked about the power of God working in us and at the crescendo, he exclaimed, "Samson was filled with the power of God and killed a thousand Philistines with the jawbone of a horse's ass!" I couldn't stop laughing!*

♪ INTENSE EMOTION SHUTS DOWN COGNITION

In a research study, participants were asked simple questions: What country do you live in? How old are you? Where were you born? Etc. Then, they were asked to go through their multiplication tables: 1 x 1 = 1, 1 x 2 = 2, etc.

Suddenly someone would slam a door behind the participant, and the participant would not "know" their multiplication tables. They would say: 6 x 1 = 6, 6 x 2 = 12, 6 x 3 (door slam) = 15, I mean 21, no wait, 18.

The participant knew what 6 x 3 was, but their thought process was affected by fear when the door slammed. When intense emotion is unprocessed, we do not know what 6 x 3 is; we do not "know" what we know. Intense emotion hinders our normal thought processing, and we appear as dumber versions of ourselves; intense emotion shuts down cognition.

LIMBIC SYSTEM

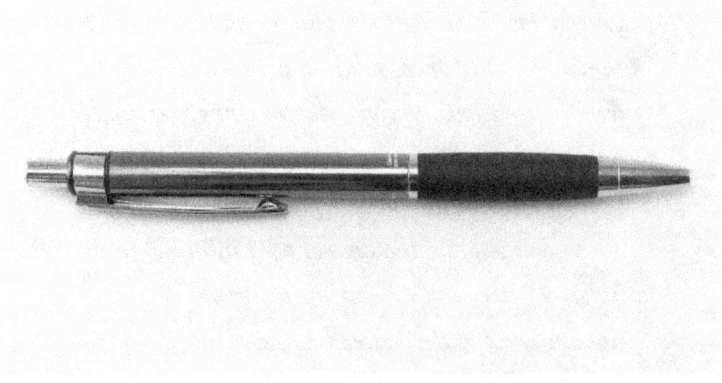

When a person sees the above picture, they 'emotion' it before they think it. In the brain, the limbic system engages before the cortexes. Emotion is processed in the limbic system; thoughts are processed in the cortexes. Emotion engages before thought, thus the emotion associated with the pen occurs before the thought associated with the pen. It's only a microsecond between the two, but the emotion is first. No one chooses to do this; it is automatic because that is how the brain is hardwired.

This is how intense emotion shuts down cognition. When intense emotion is firing in the brain, the cortexes do not engage effectively. Therefore, we think less effectively and appear as dumber versions of ourselves.

Patricia & Ken (Connection Coders):
My husband, our teenage daughter and I were returning home from a concert when Ken had to switch lanes quickly to be in the right lane for our

next turn. At the next red light, an agitated motorcyclist approached our vehicle and said Ken had cut him off and hit his motorcycle. Ken got out of the car, and the other man quickly escalated and began screaming, cursing and hitting our car. He then punched Ken, pulled out a switchblade and began waving it wildly.

I grabbed my phone and in terror began asking my daughter, "What's the number for 911?! What's the number for 911?!" She was stymied as well, as we watched Ken backing away rapidly from the attacker.

My daughter finally remembered the number. I called it and mistakenly directed the operator to send help to a completely different area of town. Fortunately, two policemen were nearby and responded quickly, prompting the knife wielding man to ride away. I was startled by the inability to remember the number for 911, as well as where we were.

This same process affects emotionally charged relational interactions and hinders connection. We all say and do things we otherwise would not say or do, things we later regret. All of us have presented less than the best version of ourselves; sometimes we are shocked by what we said or did. Many relationships suffer long term damage from something said or done in an emotionally charged moment.

THE GRACEFUL SKYDIVER

Glenn:

My first skydiving experience was exhilarating and memorable. Phyllis refused to skydive or even come to watch me; something about witnessing me splat on the ground didn't appeal to her.

Being my first skydive, it was in tandem with an instructor named Dennis. Brian, a videographer, was jumping with us to record the adventure for me.

Along with the pilot, we loaded into a plane the size of a refrigerator. Before we took off, Dennis double-checked that I was going to jump. I laughed and assured him, "Of course," along with several sentences about my unabated excitement for this experience. Because of the size of the plane and the weight of its four occupants, we gained altitude slowly, circling the drop spot endlessly. This provided extra time for the emotions to intensify.

When we reached the desired height, Brian exited the plane and held onto the wing, waiting for Dennis and me to jump. He had cameras mounted on his head and chest. Dennis and I gracefully jumped from the plane and had a delightful freefall before we pulled the ripcord to slow our descent for a lovely smooth landing.

Phyllis and our kids were excited to see the video of my experience, so we gathered in our den to watch it with popcorn and drinks at hand. Things then got wacky. As we watched the video, I was appalled to learn that the skydive company or perhaps Brian had somehow altered the video. I had shared with the fam the thrill I had experienced as Dennis and I executed a perfect 10 out of 10 swan dive out of the plane and the serenity I experienced on the descent.

However, what the video showed was a terrified newbie who had to be violently wrestled out of the plane. Dennis, who was a small man (which is preferred for tandem skydiving), repeatedly grabbed, pushed, poked, yanked, kicked and otherwise removed Glenn's hands and feet from bracing against exiting the plane. Dennis did not appear upset or unkind but was very focused on getting himself and his charge to plummet downward. When he finally accomplished this, Brian videoed a horrified hysterical screamer who would have clawed Dennis to death if he could have reached him.

To this day, I do not know how the video presented such an inaccurate version of my experience, and a starkly different (and more beautiful) memory remains with me.

Intense emotion shuts down cognition!

♪ PAIN = PAIN

Brain scanning research indicates the brain does not distinguish physical pain from emotional pain. When someone says, "I feel hurt by what you said," this is accurate. Their brain is experiencing pain as they would experience physical pain. The person is not trying to experience pain; they simply do.

In one sense, it would actually be helpful if there *was* a visible wound, because then we would be more aware of what someone is experiencing in our interactions. We would more readily realize what was happening for them and be moved to help.

Additionally, this is why someone who feels hurt by another does not want the other to touch them. The other has become a pain source, thus the brain of the one who feels hurt says, "Fear, danger, beware, pain source; you may get hurt again!" The wounded person is not trying to feel fear; they simply do.

THE NOT SO GRACEFUL NOSEDIVER

Phyllis:

I was dropping off some towels for some guests at an AirBnB, when I tripped on a step on the walkway. Not wanting to dirty or damage the towels, I held them out and away from me, resulting in my face planting on the concrete walk. The guests were coming out the door to meet me just as I fell.

A paramedic happened to be driving by just as I fell, saw me in my distress and immediately stopped to help. She also did not notice the step on the walkway, tripped on it and landed on top of me. She was not a small person, so this added considerably to my pain experience.

The guests were ladies having a 50th high school reunion and were kind and precious in caring for me. *The paramedic was unharmed, as I cushioned her fall, but such was not the case for my torso and face, which included a broken nose. While there was no permanent damage, there was lots of blood in the moment.*

The next day the pain had subsided considerably, but my face was obviously wounded and swollen. Nonetheless, it hurt mostly only when I talked or smiled. We were having several close friends over for lunch, and I told the story of what happened. These are all people who care for me deeply, but they were driven to laughter as I conveyed the story. My face hurt as I laughed with them.

Another couple arrived later, and I told the story again and experienced pain and joy again. I retold the story several more times over the ensuing days, and each retelling brought joy to me as well as the audience. As the days passed, the pain subsided then disappeared, and joy became the prominent and then the only emotion.

The retelling of the experience of physical pain does not produce more physical pain. This is not true of emotional pain. When people share stories of experiences of emotional pain, they frequently experience the emotional pain in that moment, sometimes even more intensely than they did during the original event. The emotional pain *event* occurred in the past (sometimes the distant past), but the emotional pain experience is present in the retelling.

Often someone will say (with good intent from a good heart), "That was fifteen years ago. It's in the past; let it go." But the *event* is in the past; the *experience* is in the present.

> *Telling someone to stop feeling sadness is like telling someone who's been cut to stop feeling pain. Telling them to stop crying is like telling them to stop bleeding.*

♪ CANNOT OUTLOGISTIC EMOTION

You cannot outlogisitic emotion. You will not be able to present enough facts, figures, information or content to counter the emotion a person is experiencing. (This includes your own emotion.) Attempting to outlogistic emotion is a prime example of resisting energy.

Connection Coders reference attempting to outlogistic emotion as the "court case." You might be able to convince a judge and jury that you are factually correct and win the court case, but you will lose the relationship. The goal is to win the relationship; the court case is irrelevant.

As we recognize that people are not trying to feel the emotion they feel, and as we learn to Oooo them, we make safe space for them to process emotion. Once the emotion is processed, *then* they will be able to think clearly enough to deal with the logistics. Logistics do exist, they are real, but they are not the relational issue.

This includes resisting energy by reassuring someone. If someone is feeling fear about something, telling them all the facts of why they should *not* feel fear does not help. This also disregards their experience (of the emotion), thus disregarding them. Reassuring actually makes things worse, not better.

It is important to clarify that this does not mean eliminating validation. In other words, conveying what is authentic for you after the other person processes their emotion *is* helpful. For example:

> *Wife: I feel fear that I'm not a good Mom. I don't always handle the kids as well as I should. And I feel some guilt and shame about that also sometimes.*
>
> *Husband: What? No, you're a great Mom. You're doing awesome. You don't need to feel any of that!*

OR

> *Wife: I feel fear that I'm not a good Mom. I don't always handle the kids as well as I should. And I feel some guilt and shame about that also sometimes.*
>
> *Husband: Oooo, hmmm, what happens for you with that?*
>
> *Wife: I just miss stuff with them sometimes and then I get frustrated.*
>
> *Husband: Oh wow, yeah, I get that. (After his wife has processed her emotion) Well, I feel a lot of joy about you as a Mom. I love watching you with the kids, the way you handle so much so well. Maybe we can figure out the messages of the fear, guilt and shame and make some adjustments.*

READING THROUGH THE SMOKE
CONSIDER

If you are taking an eye test, but the room is filled with smoke, you will not be able to read the eye chart. If the optometrist tells you to go ahead and read the chart and you can deal with the smoke later, this will not work. You will appear to be an illiterate person who does not even know the alphabet. You cannot read the letters until the smoke is cleared.

In the same way, unprocessed emotion 'clouds' our ability to 'see' clearly. Because the limbic system engages before the cortexes, the emotion must be processed first. Once this occurs, our cognition, thinking, reasoning and logic can engage effectively.

Phyllis (aka Honey):
We were in the car taking our grandchildren to a Christmas movie. We became aware of some escalation behind us between our two oldest grandsons, Granite (9) and his cousin Asher (8). Tuning in, we heard the following:
Granite (with intensity): Yes. I know, Asher.
Asher (excitedly): It was amazing. We couldn't believe how much candy we got!
Granite (with more intensity): Asher, I know.
Asher: I wish you had been there; it was the best Halloween ever!

Granite (voice raising): Stop talking about it!
Asher: But it was awesome. You would have loved it.
Granite (loudly and very irritated): Yes, I know. Just stop talking about it!
Honey: Granite, buddy, what's happening?
Silence from the back seat.
Honey: Hey Granite, what's happening for you?
Granite (quietly): I really wanted to go.
Honey: Oooo, go where?
Granite: I really wanted to go trick or treating with Asher, but I didn't get to. (tears forming in his eyes)

Weeks before, Granite and his siblings had planned to go trick or treating with Asher's family, but it didn't work out.

Honey: Oh wow, that stinks. So what happens for you now?
Granite: I feel really sad when Asher talks about it, cause I didn't get to go.
Honey: Mmmm, yeah, I get that.
Asher: I get that too. We don't have to talk about it. That happened for me the other day. I got up in the morning, and I couldn't find anybody in our house, so I felt a lot of guilt and shame.
Granite (contemplatively): That sounds like lonely to me and maybe fear.
Asher (laughing): Oh, yeah, I guess that would be lonely and fear.

Granite (joining in the laughter and gently teasing his cousin): Asher, you said guilt and shame.
Asher (laughing more): Yeah, that's silly.

We arrived at the movie theater, and everyone exited the vehicles and headed into the theater. Glenn and I held hands as we walked together and watched Granite and Asher laughing as they raced to the theater.

Glenn squeezed my hand and whispered, "We just changed the world, at least for those two!"

Granite and Asher sat together, shared popcorn and laughed while they watched the movie. Truly, their world had been changed.

Years ago, I would have corrected Granite about being rude to his cousin, especially because Asher was just excited to talk about his trick or treating experience. If Granite had managed to explain what was happening for him, I would have countered and attempted to explain away his experience and emotion. This would have stopped the rudeness, along with the interaction. Granite would not have felt heard, and the two would have disconnected. Because we followed Granite's energy and made safe space for him to feel *heard, he was able to process the emotion that was hindering their connection.*

CONSIDER

Mary and Beth are cooking in the kitchen. Mary accidentally knocks a large knife off the counter, and it lands on Beth's bare foot. Beth gasps from the pain and grabs her foot as it begins to bleed.

Mary: I didn't mean to do that, so don't feel pain.

Beth: Huh?! My foot's cut. It hurts like crazy, and I'm bleeding.

Mary: What? No! I didn't mean to knock the knife off the counter, so don't feel pain and don't bleed.

Beth: But I am feeling pain, and I am bleeding.

Mary: Oh, well stop, cause I didn't mean to do it.

Beth: That doesn't change the cut on my foot.

Mary: But I didn't intend to do that, so it's OK.

Beth: No, it's not OK. My foot's hurting, I'm bleeding and you're talking about your intention?!

Mary: Well yeah, it wasn't my intention to hurt you, so you shouldn't be hurt.

Beth: What are you talking about?! There's a big cut on my foot. Wow it hurts, and it's still bleeding!

Mary: Well, that's on you, cause I didn't mean to hurt you.

This scenario obviously sounds absurd, and everyone would say they would not handle it that way. However, we often do that very thing with emotional pain. If we did not *intend* for the other person to feel hurt, we often tell them *not* to feel hurt. But they are not trying to feel hurt; they simply do and telling them *not* to feel hurt does not change that. Additionally, we are disregarding their experience and emotion, thus disregarding the person, making it worse. They do not feel heard, and they lose Identity.

The reason we do this is because we are coded for empathy. We experience the emotion of those around us; we experience pain when those around us experience pain. We are also coded to eliminate pain, either by removing the pain source or removing ourselves from the pain source. Thus, we resist the energy of someone feeling pain, because we feel pain about *their* pain, and we want to eliminate it as quickly as possible.

Additionally, for most of us, when someone feels pain about something we said or did, we feel guilt or shame in addition to pain. Frequently we then attempt to explain our intentions and eliminate their emotion in an effort to *not* feel guilt and shame. It is important to wrestle through this tension to remain present with the other's pain and with our own pain. Remaining present creates safe space for the emotion to be processed and helps preserve connection.

> *Jaden (Connection Coder):*
> *I attended a Connections Codes workshop and was excited about the concepts. Although slightly skeptical, I was determined to attempt to implement quickly.*
>
> *For several months my five-year-old daughter, Wren, had been struggling with going to sleep and staying asleep, due to a fear of monsters. Each night she would convey her fear that a monster was going to get her, and I would reassure her that there were no monsters (trying to outlogistic her emotions). I would look under the bed with her, open the closet*

door and look inside with her, etc. Much to my chagrin and frustration, her fear continued unabated, and she would stay awake for long periods, frequently getting out of bed to come find me and my wife. Even after a long struggle to get to sleep, she would awaken through the night and then awaken us. Sleep deprivation had become the household norm, along with its ramifications.

The evening after the Connection Codes workshop, I was putting Wren to bed, and she began her nightly routine of talking about her fear of monsters. I determined to follow her energy, not try to outlogistic her emotion and Oooo her instead. And this happened:

Wren: Daddy, what if a monster tries to get me?!
Me: Oooo, wow, yeah, what happens for you when you think about that?
Wren: I get so scared; I'm always scared!
Me: Mmmm, yeah I get that. That would be scary! I remember feeling scared like that too, when I was little.

I began to relate a story to her about being scared when I was a little boy, when I heard her breathing deeply. I trailed off my story as I realized my little girl was asleep. I laid there a few minutes, enjoying the sound of her restful slumber and being mesmerized by what had just happened.

For many months I had resisted Wren's energy and tried to outlogistic her emotion. While it was from a good heart with great intentions, this had actually exacerbated the situation, making life worse. Once I followed her energy, regarded her emotion and made safe space for it, she was able to process the emotion, feel heard and sleep. She slept through the night, and we awakened the next morning after a full night's sleep excited about the possibility of this being our new lifestyle!

> **People can process logistics once they process emotion.**
> **They cannot process emotion if they simply process logistics.**

43 FEET

If you were sitting outside in a folding chair and the chair was raised a foot off the ground, you'd be fine. If the chair was raised to five feet off the ground, you would begin experiencing fear, as you thought, "If I fall out of this chair, . . . " Measurements of your fear level could be monitored by the rate of your heart beat, breathing and sweating. If the chair was raised to ten feet, those rates would continue to escalate.

Research has shown that, on average, the fear experience maximizes around 43 feet. After that height, your rates do not continue to increase, even if you are raised to 100 feet or more. You will not be petrified times two or terrified + 57. You are maxed out; you are simply terrified. As it relates to emotion, there are two important aspects of the 43 feet concept.

First: Your experience is your experience. Your emotion is your emotion. Your trauma is your trauma.

If you were at 43 feet and you were told that another person is at 100 feet and he's terrified, therefore you can only be half of terrified, you would say, "What are you talking about? I'm terrified." This is why being told children are starving in India does not help with the experience of eating Brussel sprouts. If you are told people around the world are being shot at, that does not help your stress level about your finances. Another's experience has no effect on your experience.

This is equally true with trauma. If we are in a therapy session with someone who lost a leg, we would help them process their trauma. If someone then came in who lost two legs, we would not turn to the first person and say, "Your trauma is only half of this person's trauma, because one is half of two." Then if someone came in who lost two legs, an arm and an eye, we would not say to the first person, "Your trauma is only about nineteen percent of that person's trauma." The first person would not be benefited by such a comparison. The other person's experience and trauma has no bearing on the first person's experience and trauma.

Your experience is your experience. Your emotion is your emotion. Your trauma is your trauma.

Second: The goal is to process emotion well below 43 feet. Connection Coders use this as a reference point. For example:

Lucy: I'm feeling fear about my presentation at work tomorrow.

> Scott: Oooo, what's happening with that? Like 43 feet of fear?
> Lucy: No, probably about eight feet.
> Scott: Oooo, yeah, OK, I get that.

As emotion escalates, we struggle to function sensibly. If someone was raised to 43 feet in the air, they might become hysterical to the point of falling out of the chair, causing the very harm they feared. This is true of all the core emotions. Intense emotion shuts down cognition, and we function as dumber versions of ourselves. Thus, it is vital to process emotion long before 43 feet!

Although research shows that the fear of heights maximizes at 43 feet, it is the same region of the brain firing for lesser levels of fear. In other words, 43 feet of fear might be identified as terrified or petrified, while less intense fear might be labeled uncertain, hesitant, apprehensive, nervous, etc. Degradation might be viewed as 43 feet of shame, whereas insecurity might be six feet. Regardless, the same area of the brain is activating.

> *A human can easily stand on a one foot square board. Raising that board into the air completely changes that experience, despite the size of the board remaining exactly the same!*

THE RIVER OF EMOTION
CONSIDER

You're sitting beside a river on a warm summer day: feet in the cool water, birds chirping, frogs croaking, turtles turtling, snakes slithering (Delete snakes from the scene, if you don't like them). The water is refreshing, and the setting brings peace and serenity. You are not concerned with how much water is passing by; you do not count the gallons.

Suddenly, an evil ogre builds a dam downstream, and water begins backing up. The quantity of water is an immediate issue. What was bringing goodness moments before is now a danger, threatening your safety as well as the safety of those closest to you and, ultimately, your entire community.

The water in this analogy is emotion. As long as the River of Emotion is flowing, it doesn't matter how many gallons of emotion there are. The flowing emotion brings refreshment, peace and serenity. When emotion is dammed, the quantity of emotion is an immediate issue; what is designed to bring goodness now is a danger, threatening your safety, as well as the safety of those closest to you and ultimately your entire community.

The goal is for the River of Emotion to flow freely, to be refreshing and bring peace and serenity. For this to happen, dams need to burst. A word of warning: when a dam bursts, there is a massive torrent of gushing water, and you have to hold on for dear life for a bit until the river settles down. It will settle down, but it might be a frightening scenario.

In the same way, when a dam is removed from the River of Emotion, there is a torrent of gushing emotion, and you may have to hold on for dear life. It will settle down, it will be a river soon, but it might be a frightening scenario for a bit.

As long as the river flows freely, emotion brings richness to life. Damage occurs when the River of Emotion is dammed. When a dam bursts, it can be scary, but we will get through it, and the River will calm and return to its life-giving role.

Josie & Will (Connection Coders):
Josie: After several weeks of learning the Connection Codes, I began to open up with Will. I began to realize the deep hurts I had experienced in our relationship. During one session, which was such a turning point for us, I got so flooded, I began yelling repeatedly, "You ruined my life! You ruined my life! You ruined my life!" I was so out of control, as the hurt flooded every fiber of my being.
Will: I didn't know what to do. I was so overwhelmed!
Josie: And I didn't care because I was overwhelmed too.
Will: I looked over at our therapist for help, and he said, "A dam's bursting; just hold on for dear life. It'll be a river soon."
Josie: It's so weird, cause I didn't even hear him say that, but Will was able to just Oooo me, just hear me, just be present with me. I'm so embarrassed with how out of control I was. I said so many unkind, unfair things.
Will: It was intense, but I'm so glad she was able to process all that. She so desperately needed to. We

> both know she was inaccurate with some of it, but it helped me see how big it was for her.
> Josie: Now, I tell him in the moment, as it happens. No dams!
> Will: And I love it!

Most catastrophic human interactions occur because of an emotional dam. The horrific stories you hear in the news about what someone did to another is the result of an emotional dam, an unprocessed emotion. People don't commit atrocities because of two feet of emotion. they do it from 43 feet of emotion, an emotional buildup, an emotional dam.

> *Live a dam free life;*
> *let the River flow!*

ONE POUND WEIGHT

If you hand someone a one pound weight, they can handle it. If you ask them to set it over there, they can handle it. If you do this 500 times over the course of a month, they can handle it. At the end of the month, you might say, "Wow, that was 500 pounds of stuff!" Neither of you noticed, because you handled it one pound at a time. If you waited until the end of the month and handed them 500 pounds, they would notice; they would be crushed. They can handle one pound 500 times; they cannot handle 500 pounds one time.

If you hand someone 'one pound' of emotion, they can handle it. If you ask them to help you process it, they can handle it. If you do this 500 times over the course of a month, they can handle it. At the end of the month, you might say, "Wow, that was 500 pounds of emotion." Neither of you noticed, because you handled it one pound at a time. If you waited until the end of the month and handed them 500 pounds, they would notice; they would be crushed. They can handle one pound 500 times; they cannot handle 500 pounds one time.

When we process emotion as it happens (one pound at a time), it is manageable. When we try to handle 500 pounds of emotion, it is crushing. When we were babies, we processed emotion as it happened (one pound at a time). This is how we are coded, which did not change just because we got older.

1ST TIME, EVERY TIME, ANYTIME, ALL THE TIME…AS INSTANTLY AS POSSIBLE

To live a dam free life and let the River of Emotion flow freely, we must manage emotion one pound at a time, conveying emotion the first time, every time, anytime, all the time, as instantly as possible. We did this perfectly as infants, because this is how we are coded. We never got recoded; we simply got reprogrammed by interactions, situations, events, circumstances, etc. We learned *not* to process the first time, every time, anytime, all the time, as instantly as possible.

A caveat: as adults, we have responsibilities that sometimes prevent processing with another in the moment. Nevertheless, especially in long term relationships of depth, the goal is to process emotion in the moment as much as possible.

Another component of *not* processing the first time, every time, anytime, all the time is the pain the other person in a relationship experiences when they find out there has not been authenticity. This creates more disconnection and adds another dam that must burst to establish deep connection. In response to a dam bursting, we often hear something like, "What?! You mean you've been telling me everything was OK all this time, but it wasn't?!" When we convey emotion the first time, every time, anytime, all the time, as instantly as possible, there are no dams that need to burst, and the hurt that the other will experience in finding out about the dam will not occur.

> *Glenn: I did not trust Phyllis an hour before I met her, because I did not trust anyone. I did not feel safe with her even before I met her, because I did not feel safe with anyone. We were twenty years into our relationship before she discovered this heart wrenching information. She was devastated when she realized the pain and difficulty that came from me not conveying what was authentic.*
>
> *Phyllis: I spent endless time not knowing what was happening with my partner. I cared so much for him but had no idea how to connect with him. When we finally were able to achieve some authenticity, it was so sad to learn of the fear he experienced with me, but even sadder to realize this had been true for many years.*
>
> *Glenn: Now I just tell her what's happening with me.*
>
> *Phyllis: And, I love it, so simple and so connecting.*

> *Glenn: That does not mean I don't still feel fear with her at times. She is incredibly safe for me, but that doesn't mean I feel safe with her. The difference is now I just tell her. Also, she knows that my fear is just my fear. She may or may not have done anything to contribute to it. She realizes this has nothing to do with Phyllis, even if it looks like it's all about Phyllis. Either way, I just process it with her.*
>
> *Phyllis: Also, when he processes the fear, that does not mean he will not feel fear again in ten minutes or an hour or tomorrow. He'll process the fear then as well. There is no quota or limit on how many times we are allowed to experience an emotion.*
>
> *Glenn: Which is how we are coded. Hopefully you would never say to a baby, "You felt sad earlier, so you're not allowed to feel sad now." The baby is experiencing what the baby is experiencing, and it is important that they convey that.*

PULLING AWAY AND PUSHING AWAY IS THE SAME DISTANCE.

Physically or emotionally pushing someone away from you obviously causes disconnect. If you yell at someone, "Get away from me," and shove them, the two of you will disconnect. Everyone knows that.

However, when we emotionally *pull* away from others, the same disconnect occurs. When we do not convey what is happening within us authentically, the other person experiences us pulling away.

Many of us often think that *not* conveying emotion to another is good and helpful. We think we're protecting the other person by *not* telling them what is happening. We don't convey what is happening authentically, out of protection of connection or prevention of disconnection. With good intention, we pull away, thinking we are doing what is best for the relationship. But the other person in the situation experiences the same distance as if they had been pushed away. Pulling away and pushing away is the same distance.

Also, living inauthentically becomes extremely difficult. We may be able to do so temporarily, but ultimately the other knows something is amiss. Additionally, when someone is not sure what is happening, they will fill in the blanks. This further threatens connection, because the filled in blanks are usually inaccurate and detrimental. For example:

He's probably being quiet because he's mad at me.
I bet she's not talking to me because she regrets marrying me. She probably wishes she married that other guy from high school.
I wonder if he's upset because I forgot to do what I told him I'd do.

Lindsey & Rob (Connection Coders):
Lindsey: I've been amazed at the difference it makes for our connection when Rob tells me what's happening with him. He has a really stressful job,

and he used to come home and be quiet, which felt cold and distant to me.

Rob: I wouldn't tell her about my day, because I didn't want to stress her out. We have five children, and she's with them all day. So I felt I was doing good by not telling her my stress. I thought it would just add to her stress. I thought it would make things harder for her, especially if my day didn't go well.

Lindsey: But, what was happening for me was I thought he didn't like me, that he didn't want to be with me, as well as the kids.

Rob: I'd come home and say I needed time to unwind and that could end up being hours, and I still didn't feel good. My stress would just be to a manageable level.

Lindsey: At one point, I accused him of having an affair because we were so disconnected!

Rob: I was stunned by that, because I was barely surviving. I was so offended by her accusation, because I was trying so hard to take care of our family, and again, I thought I was helping by not telling her how stressed I was.

Lindsey: Now, he comes home, and we process our emotions together, takes a few minutes, totally different world!

Rob: I had no idea how simple it could be and that what I was doing to try to help was actually hurting.

Lindsey: We're living a dam free life, the River of Emotion is flowing, and we're loving it!

Kristina (Connection Coder):
My husband and I have three children, and we adore all three of them. I got pregnant with our fourth and all five of us were so excited about this new addition. I then had a miscarriage, and we processed through the intense sadness of that experience as a family. I saw the pain my children experienced as we cried together. I got pregnant again, and we decided not to tell the kids at first in case something went wrong. It did, and we lost that baby also.

At that point, we told our children the sad news. Our children felt hurt that we had not told them about the pregnancy. We explained that we did not tell them, because we did not want them to be disappointed. Our oldest, a ten-year-old son and a Connection Coder extraordinaire said, "Mom, we can handle disappointment; we just want to be with you!" We then shared tears of joy and sadness together.

Wow! They get it! We are more open than ever as a family, and our teamship is amazing!

3 SENTENCES

As previously covered, emotion makes us aware of needs, serving to protect us. This includes helping to connect us, as we are stronger in teamship. We are coded to convey the message of the emotion in order to get help. The message we are coded to convey can be summed up in three sentences:

>I feel (core emotion).
>
>I need _____.
>
>Will you help me?

No one wonders what is happening with a ten-month-old. Everyone knows because the baby continually makes it clear. This is automatic. They are coded this way, and it is vital for their health and survival. Babies convey emotion prompted by needs and seek connection in that experience.

This is not a conscious plan. Babies do not awaken each morning and determine to convey the needs that emotion brought to their attention. Also, they never awaken at 3:00 in the morning with fear, loneliness, pain or hunger and decide to wait until 7:00 to let someone know about it. They never think, "My parents are probably tired, so I won't bother them right now. I'll let them know what was happening with me when they awaken."

The need to convey the message of these three sentences does not change as we get older. We are simply older babies who need to *feel* heard as we convey these three sentences. (Infants demand help; as adults we need to ask.) This facilitates our health and our very survival.

The goal with these three sentences is to help us function as we are coded to function. The goal is to convey the message of the emotion to those around us, so as to get the help we need.

This leads to the fourth phrase: When someone is able to convey the three sentences automatically, according to their coding, communication and connection is smooth and easy. However, most of us do this poorly. Thus, we add a fourth phrase to "Oooo.

What happens? I missed it." Asking "How can I help?" further invites someone into their own experience and helps them convey their need. The three sentences will eventually become automatic, and the fourth phrase is very powerful in facilitating that.

A CUP OF TEA AND ME

Glenn: The three sentences simply yet powerfully facilitate our connection. Now I'm able to be authentic and convey, "I'm feeling lonely."

Phyllis: To which I respond, "Oooo, what's happening with lonely? What am I missing?"

Glenn: And I tell her, "I miss you. Seems like we haven't had much time together lately, and I really want to be with you."

Phyllis: And then I get it. I understand what's happening with him. Also, I receive Identity; I feel valued and special.

Glenn: And, I feel heard.

Phyllis: Often I'm in the middle of something and can't stop immediately, but I'll say, "Oooo, wow, OK, how can I help with that? Maybe a cup of tea when I finish with this."

Glenn: And I'll say, "Yeah, like a really big one with scalding water!"

Phyllis: That whole interaction takes a few seconds and is very connecting!

SECTION 2 TAKEAWAYS

Emotion is a human right. Humans experience 8 core emotions.

Emotion serves a purpose: to protect and connect us.

Communicate the core emotion, not *through* the emotion.

Humans connect through emotion, not logistics.

Every emotion is an opportunity to connect.

Emotion happens to you. You're responsible for the next action.

Intense emotion shuts down cognition. The limbic system engages before the cortexes.

The brain does not distinguish physical and emotional pain.

You cannot outlogistic emotion, regardless of intention.

Your experience is your experience; your emotion is your emotion; trauma is trauma.

Live a dam free life; let the River flow.

Pulling away and pushing away is the same distance.

The 3 sentences: I feel _____. I need _____. Will you help me?

The 4 phrases: Oooo. What happens? I missed it. How can I help/what do you need?

Glenn is not a very good skydiver, but he loves having a cup of tea with Phyllis.

Following are Core Emotion Experience Assignments 1 and 2. Complete assignment 1 before continuing with assignment 2. Be sure to take the time to do the Experience Assignments, because the power of the Connection Codes is not in the content but in the experience.

Remember that Oooo is always the correct response. Some sharing will not be clear or make sense to the listener. Nonetheless, making safe space for the other is crucial!

CORE EMOTION EXPERIENCE ASSIGNMENT 1

What did I understand about emotion as a child?

What did I learn to do with my emotion?

How did I learn to respond to others' emotions?

How do I typically respond to emotion now?

CORE EMOTION EXPERIENCE ASSIGNMENT 2

The core emotion I experience the most is

The emotion I have the most difficulty sharing is

An example of a time I communicated *through* emotion:

An example of a time I experienced 43 feet of emotion:

When I get dammed up, I tend to

An example of a time I pushed away: pulled away:

Section 2
Focus

Notice emotion and tune into its message. Process with someone you trust by using the three sentences:

>   I feel _____.
>   I need _____.
>   Will you help me?

Follow the energy of those around you, and help them tune into the message of emotion using the three sentences:

>   What (emotion) happens for you there?
>   What do you need?
>   How can I help?

SECTION 3

Core Emotion Wheel

Because emotion is designed to help us and we need that help, it is important that it accomplishes its purpose. Recognizing the difficulty most of us have processing emotion, we developed the Core Emotion Wheel (CEW). It's called a wheel because it is designed to transport us into deep connection and move us to be the best version of ourselves.

The Core Emotion Wheel experience is simple, brief and directional. For some people, it is easy and automatic. For others, it is challenging and even painful. Regardless, when employed consistently, it assists with processing emotion and connecting us, helping to make us the best possible version of ourselves.

Now, let's expound on the eight core emotions in conjunction with the Core Emotion Wheel.

PLEASURE CENTER: JOY

The brain's reward system is composed of pleasure centers or hedonic hotspots. These are responsible for producing the neurotransmitter dopamine, the 'feel good' hormone, which results in a pleasurable sensation a.k.a. joy. This sends a message that what is happening is desirable and worth repeating. Consistent dopamine production is crucial in the human experience, as a deficiency of dopamine is detrimental and potentially catastrophic.

Joy is in the middle of the Wheel because the other emotions center around it and help facilitate it. Virtually all human behavior is influenced by the pleasure center; whether by the experience of joy or the lack of it. Innumerable activities are motivated by our dopamine quest. The other core emotions serve to help us by protecting, facilitating and maximizing our joy experience, thereby enriching our lives.

The effect of our dopamine quest is endless and includes:
What we eat.
What we wear.
Where we live.
What we do: jobs, travel, activities, hobbies, etc.
Who we spend time with.
The music we listen to.
The temperature we set on the thermostat.

The danger of unprocessed joy is pursuing things that will ultimately be a detriment. Unprocessed joy often overrides other core emotions that are trying to send an important message. For example, people often buy something they cannot afford because they are flooded with joy about that item. They do not notice the fear message that it is out of their budget or the guilt message that buying that item is irresponsible. All of us have made decisions from joy that ended up being a detriment.

The dopamine quest is significant in the human experience and affects each of us continuously. The key is to process the joy, so we can determine the best course of action and make the best decision.

ANGER: PRIMARY & SECONDARY

The brain's anger response occurs predominantly in the amygdala, a key component of the limbic system. This is responsible for producing the neurotransmitter epinephrine, commonly referenced as adrenaline, which results in an increase of energy and strength. This sends a message that what you are experiencing is important and needs focus. This is often referenced as the fight or flight response. Anger serves as a driving force to accomplish what needs to be accomplished. Consistent epinephrine production is crucial in the human experience, as a deficiency of epinephrine is detrimental and potentially catastrophic.

Anger is at the top of the Wheel because it is so prominent in influencing human behavior both positively and negatively. Anger is our strongest as well as our longest motivator. People do intense and amazing things, both positive and negative, when pushed by anger.

Anger looks blurry on the Wheel because there are two of them, primary anger and secondary anger. Also, anger is most often the core emotion that blurs our thinking, resulting in poor decisions and behavior. Thus, it is accurate when someone says, "I was so mad I couldn't think straight."

Secondary anger is called second because another core emotion occurred first; a different core emotion preceded it. If someone feels hurt by what another person said, anger might activate. This would be secondary anger. Pain (hurt) occurred first; anger occurred second. Pain happened before the anger. On a brain scan, a freeze frame would show pain, pain, pain/anger, pain/anger, etc. Often, there is only a microsecond between, but the pain is first. The anger is second (thus secondary). For example:

> *Paul is meeting a group of friends for lunch. When he approaches the table, Thomas sarcastically says, "Nice jacket."*

> Paul responds, "Who made you the fashion police? Sorry I didn't call you to get your input on what I should wear! Besides, look at what you're wearing. Is that your t-shirt from junior high school?!"
> Paul is showing anger, but he initially felt hurt. (He may also have felt embarrassed/shame.) Again, it might seem instant, but the anger occurred after a different core emotion.

Important point: primary and secondary anger appear the same on a brain scan. Secondary anger is not artificial, substitute or discounted anger. It *is* anger, but it was preceded and triggered by a core emotion.

Most anger in personal interactions is secondary and does not lead to connection. For relational connection, we need to find out what happened *before* the secondary anger to identify the first *core* emotion because humans connect through conveying *core* emotions.

If Paul and Thomas are implementing the Connection Codes, the interaction would be more like:

> *Thomas (sarcastically): Nice jacket.*
> *Paul: Oooo, that feels painful, kinda hurts.*
> *Thomas: Oooo, what just happened?*
> *Paul: Mmm, felt painful that you're insulting my jacket.*
> *Thomas: Oh, I get that. Yeah, I shouldn't have said that. Feel some guilt.*
> *Paul: Oooo yeah, OK.*

Primary anger in interactions is often about someone else's situation. You might experience core level anger when you hear about something horrific that happened to another person. You are not feeling anger on your own behalf, but anger is activated by the situation on behalf of another.

Additionally, anger is a powerful driver and core level anger pushes us towards achievement. Nothing great was ever accomplished without core level anger. This includes:

completing a marathon long after the body says "Stop!"

completing a project long after the body says "Sleep!"

developing a solution to help people in their struggles.

standing up for another person being treated unfairly.

pushing beyond exhaustion to help someone in need.

The danger of unprocessed anger, particularly secondary, is the damaging decisions we make in response to it. As previously stated, we often do not think clearly when flooded with anger, and we make poor decisions. All of us have said and done harmful things to ourselves and others out of anger. Also, unprocessed anger results in excess adrenaline, which is extremely damaging to the body.

Anger is significant in the human experience and affects each of us continuously. The key is to process the anger so we can determine the best course of action and make the best decision.

DISGUST: GUILT & SHAME

Scientifically, the brain's disgust response is the least understood of the core emotions. Disgust seems to occur primarily in the insula and is at least loosely associated with pain, fear and anger. The message of disgust is that something is undesirable (pain), could cause harm (fear) and should be avoided (anger). This can be associated with physical, behavioral or social sources. The experience of disgust is crucial in the human experience, as a deficiency of disgust is detrimental and potentially catastrophic.

There are not distinguishable differences on a brain scan between guilt and shame. However, they are separate on the Wheel because of the difference in how people experience them, including facial and bodily reactions along with behavioral response. Typically, guilt involves external; shame involves internal.

Guilt is about what I did; shame is about who I am. Guilt is about one's action; shame is about one's essence and is very Identity oriented. Shame is the most dangerous of the core emotions. Unprocessed shame becomes toxic and can have devastating effect.

There is considerable messaging in our culture that labels guilt and shame as bad. Guilt and shame are not bad; they help you see detrimental behavior. *Unprocessed* guilt and shame are bad, but that's true of every emotion. A guilt and shame free person is a sociopath; we don't need more sociopaths!

Guilt messages us that we made a mistake and need to do something differently next time. Without guilt, a child would not learn that 5+5 does not equal 55. It looks like it could, but when the child is corrected, the child experiences guilt and learns that 5+5=10. In the same way, when we behave poorly with one another, guilt activates us to change our behavior next time. Without guilt, we repeat the same detrimental behavior, and our relationships are damaged and unravel. Guilt is crucial for deep connection!

Shame is presented on the Wheel as SHAme, showing 'the

little me.' Shame's message conveys, "You are being a lesser version of yourself; you need to do better." Shame helps us monitor our behavior and helps prevent damage. This includes:

>*not producing socially inappropriate gestures and bodily sounds.*
>
>*dressing appropriately.*
>
>*not making inappropriate comments.*

It is important to remember that emotion is our consultant rather than our dictator. We need to process emotion to glean the message and determine what is best to do next.

A danger of unprocessed guilt is not learning from mistakes. Guilt helps us learn, develop and grow. A lack of guilt is damaging to connection, as the other person loses Identity when the same detrimental behavior is repeated. Also, unprocessed guilt becomes overwhelming and defeating resulting in us giving up or not even trying. When we process guilt, we realize that we simply missed something; it is manageable to try again and improve.

Shame is the most dangerous of the core emotions. Danger is neutral, not good or bad, positive or negative. Something that is dangerous requires special focus; such is the case with shame. Unprocessed shame becomes toxic, as it is especially Identity oriented. Unprocessed shame leads to the individual feeling like the 'little me,' having less and less Identity, resulting in messages like:

>*I am bad.*
>
>*I am worthless.*
>
>*I am useless.*
>
>*I have no value.*
>
>*I do not matter.*

When we process shame, we can evaluate the message and determine what adjustments need to be made to be the best versions of ourselves.

Guilt and shame are significant in the human experience and affect each of us continuously. The key is to process them, so we can determine the best course of action and make the best decision.

FEAR

The brain's fear response seems to begin in the thalamus and amygdala but involves chemical and electrical charges of a series of networks throughout the brain and body. This begins with our most prevalent neurotransmitter glutamate then involves dozens of other chemicals including cortisol, epinephrine, glucose and oxytocin. This process alerts then preps us for a potential threat conveying a message of "Danger; beware and prepare!" As Chip Dodd says in *Voice of the Heart*, fear awakens us to danger. This helps modulate our behavior to ensure our safety and survival. Consistent fear is crucial in the human experience, as a deficiency of fear is detrimental and potentially catastrophic.

Fear is the fastest activating of the core emotions and usually the fastest dissipating. If we hear an explosion, we instantly feel fear but then the fear quickly subsides. We don't think for a minute and then react; we react instantly then the fear fades. Also, we don't wait an hour and then feel fear. If we are still reacting after the fear causing stimulus is gone, that is called trauma or post-traumatic stress disorder (PTSD).

There is much in our culture that says fear is bad and that we should ignore or overcome it. Fear is not bad; it helps us recognize threats and be prepared to manage them.

Fear . . .
> *keeps people in their lane while driving; it's not those dotted white lines.*
> *keeps people from walking off the edge of a cliff.*
> *helps people use dangerous equipment safely.*
> *keeps people from driving north on the southbound side of the interstate.*
> *alerts us not to say harmful things to others.*

The danger of unprocessed fear is that it hinders us from constructive choices and actions. Each of us has not attempted something that needed to be done because fear blocked us from doing so. Also, each of us has done actions due to unprocessed fear that were a detriment to ourselves or others. Additionally, unprocessed fear results in excess cortisol, which becomes extremely damaging to the body.

Fear is significant in the human experience and affects each of us continuously. The key is to process it so we can determine the best course of action and make the best decision.

> *A fear free person soon will be a dead person!*

PAIN: HURT, SAD, LONELY

The brain processes pain through the spinal cord and then the anterior cingulate. Different types of fibers result in different speeds and intensity of a pain experience, but they all convey a message that harm is occurring. Consistent pain messaging is crucial in the human experience, as a deficiency of it is detrimental and potentially catastrophic.

Emotional pain is divided into three categories: hurt, sad and lonely. Brain scanning imagery as well as affective (external) factors, such as facial, bodily and behavioral reactions, help differentiate these three. There is considerable difference in how we respond to hurt, sad and lonely.

Hurt is an acute or sharp stabbing pain and appears on a brain scan like a firework display. When someone feels physical hurt, they react instantly and aggressively to disconnect from the pain source, either by removing it or moving away from it. When someone feels emotional hurt, they react instantly and aggressively to disconnect from the pain source, either by removing it or moving away from it. When someone feels emotionally hurt by another, they frequently will recoil if the other person reaches to touch them. Because the brain does not distinguish physical and emotional pain, the brain messages, "Beware of pain source; they may hurt you again."

Sad is less acute and intense than hurt but more sustained and permeating. The instantaneous reaction does not occur, and the pain experience is longer. Different than with hurt, how to eliminate the pain often is not as obvious and automatic. Sad alerts us to what is valuable and worth pursuing and, conversely, what is important to change or eliminate.

Lonely is a dull, aching, chronic pain without peaks but slower activating and longer than hurt or sad. Lonely reminds us of our coded need for deep connection and presses us to pursue and maintain connection.

Longitudinal and disparate research studies indicate that living lonely is more damaging than smoking a pack of cigarettes a day! That says if someone lives in deep connection and smokes a pack of cigarettes a day, they are better off than if they live in disconnection but never smoke. It is not the goal to get people to smoke cigarettes, but that is remarkable! As a society, we have gone to extensive efforts to get people to stop smoking. In a shop at a port in the Caribbean, the *front* of packs of cigarettes state in bold letters, "This will kill you!" Equal efforts are needed to help people not live in disconnection. Also, the occurrence rates of catastrophic health events, such as heart attacks and strokes, increase markedly when we are alone.

UCLA researcher Dr Steve Cole presents, "We're highly dependent on others from birth. Humans aren't like other animals. We're not that big, we're not that strong, and we don't have big, long teeth. The way we've come to rule the world is by banding together in groups, which are capable of doing things that no one of us by ourselves could do. Our survival and thriving depends on being part of a community. When we fall out of that sense of connection and community, our bodies respond to that as if we were literally threatened."

Cole further emphasizes, "Loneliness acts as a fertilizer for other diseases. The biology of loneliness can accelerate the buildup of plaque in arteries, help cancer cells grow and spread, and promote inflammation in the brain leading to Alzheimer's disease. Loneliness promotes several different types of wear and tear on the body."

The danger of unprocessed pain is the continuing damage from the pain source, as well as a lack of adjusting to prevent future harm.

Pain, both physical and emotional, is significant in the human experience and affects each of us continuously. The key is to process it, so we can determine the best course of action and make the best decision.

> *Phyllis:*
> *Sad for me often comes in a cloud, and I don't always know what's happening with the sad. Sometimes, I just wake up with it. I feel heavy; the cloud surrounds me. I tell Glenn about the sad even though I can't always figure out the source. Just telling him leads to the sadness dissipating and helps me to stay connected with him.*

Many people ask why the Core Emotion Wheel has seven negative emotions and only one positive emotion (joy). First, understand that we did not create the core emotions; this is simply the human condition. None of us decided how the human brain would function. We did not choose what the brain would do and how it would do it. The Connection Codes simply report and reflect on research. Second, emotions are neither positive or negative, good or bad, right or wrong. Emotions simply are; they simply occur. The danger and damage is in not processing emotion.

For example, most people think of joy as positive, but joy can be extremely detrimental. Cocaine addiction develops because of joy. Cocaine usage inhibits the reuptake of dopamine in the brain, maximizing the joy experience. The individual experiences a euphoric sensation and receives the message to repeat that experience. When the individual does so again and again, they become a cocaine addict. This is facilitated by unprocessed joy. Each of us, at times, behaves detrimentally due to joy. Everyone has eaten poorly, overspent, under exercised, binged watched or countless other behaviors due to joy, but that does not mean joy is bad or negative. Emotion is not positive or negative. Un*processed* emotion is the problem.

> *Why are there 8 core emotions (or 5 emotion regions in the brain?) The same reason there are 3 primary colors (red, blue and yellow)- there just are.*

Emotion is the universal language of human connection, so becoming proficient at processing emotion is crucial for deep connection. The Core Emotion Wheel is the tool being used around the world to facilitate this.

> *The Core Emotion Wheel is not the goal-*
> *it is a tool, a means to an end.*
> *The goal is processing emotion in real time.*

Following are instructions for using the Core Emotion Wheel. Be sure to take the time to do the experience assignments because the power of the Connection Codes is not in the content but in the experience.

THE CORE EMOTION WHEEL EXPERIENCE INSTRUCTIONS

Place the Core Emotion Wheel (CEW) where each can see it, but do not hold it.

Speak directly to each other, maintaining eye contact as much as possible. With one or two sentences, convey a recent experience involving a core emotion. If nothing recent comes to mind, share the last time that emotion happened. If not the last time, then share a 'big' time, perhaps something from childhood.

If you are the listener, respond only with a version of Oooo.

The more authentic the sharing is, the better. However, any sharing, even if it is inaccurate, needs only an Oooo in response.

After one shares all eight core emotions (don't forget Joy), reverse roles and repeat.

The CEW experience takes 4 minutes or less. (8 emotions X 15 seconds each X 2 people = 4 minutes.)

The goal is to retrain your brain to share core emotions proficiently.

It is important that the CEW experience is brief (four minutes or less) so that your brain experiences it as simple and doable, rather than long and arduous (e.g. painful), because we are coded to avoid pain. Brevity is crucial because the goal is to do the CEW experience every day. If it takes four minutes, this is implementable. Research shows that more than four minutes greatly reduces the chances of daily repetition.

For many of us, the idea of doing the CEW every day sounds daunting. Bear in mind, there are numerous activities we do every day. Connection Coders say, "Brush your teeth every day; do the Core Emotion Wheel every day." If you have to choose between the two, do the CEW (but only for one day; we don't want to be responsible for you getting cavities!)

The goal of doing the Wheel every day underscores the importance of it taking four minutes or less. Most people live busy lives and find it difficult to incorporate a 10+ minute exercise. Many people find themselves tired and spent at the end of a day. Nonetheless, when they know the Wheel is brief, they can say, "We forgot to do the Wheel. Well, it'll just take four minutes, so let's do it."

Another point about doing the Wheel consistently is that we have received countless ongoing messages for most of our lives *not* to process emotion. We have been programmed *not* to be authentic, *not* to convey what is happening at our core. We have been brainwashed, and it will take considerable intentional concerted effort to get *un*brainwashed.

EATING ROACHES

Glenn:
I do not normally eat roaches. I ate one in high

> *school for $1; I was very poor then. I also ate a cigarette for $1. If you ever have to choose between eating a roach or a cigarette, choose the roach. I was sick for several days after I ate the cigarette. Apparently, there are ingredients in cigarettes that are not beneficial for the human digestive tract.*

For many cultures, the idea of eating a roach is repulsive. However, some cultures around the world are puzzled by our reticence *not* to eat roaches. Some cultures enjoy eating them and recognize them as an excellent source of protein. When prepared properly, they can be delectable and nutritious. Nonetheless, for many of us, it would be quite an endeavor to eat roaches and, further still, to enjoy eating them.

How long would it take for you to become proficient at eating roaches? You have received so much influence *not* to eat roaches that it might be arduous to get you to enjoy eating them. Again, not just eating a roach for a dollar ($4 when adjusted for inflation), but to regularly enjoy eating them. We have been brainwashed *not* to eat roaches.

In the same way, most of us have been brainwashed *not* to process emotion. We have received so much influence *not* to process emotion that it may be challenging to become proficient at it. This is why we do the CEW endlessly; we are going against so much cultural training *not* to be authentic. We were born and are coded to be authentic but have been reprogrammed by interactions, events, situations, circumstances, etc. We never were recoded, but we have been reprogrammed. Growing into this may not be automatic or easy, but it is simple.

BROKEN EXERCISE EQUIPMENT

Glenn:

On my first day at the gym after far too long of an absence, I sat down at a machine that is similar to a recumbent bike, except more of a stepping motion than pedaling. The resistance level could be set from 1 to 20, in one-tenth increments. Trying to be realistic, I opted for a low setting to begin. My favorite number is four, so I opted for a setting of 4.4. Apparently, something was jammed or broken on the mechanism because the foot pieces would not move when I pushed on them. I went to get help.

Glenn (to fitness center staff member): Excuse me. The machine I'm trying to use is broken.

Seth (staff member): Oh my, OK, I'll come take a look. (sitting on the machine and effortlessly pressing the pedals, which immediately and smoothly moved back and forth): Hmmm, well, it seems to be OK.

Glenn: Oh great, you got it working.

Seth (standing up): Yeah, you should be good to go.

Glenn (sitting on the machine and vigorously pressing on the pedals, which did not move): Well dang, it won't move for me. Wonder what's wrong with it.

Seth: Let's try something here. (Adjusting setting to 0.2, not 2.0 but 0.2) Try that.

Glenn (again pressing vigorously on the pedals and able to move them slowly): Well dang.

> *Another time I was at the gym and following behind a petite elderly woman on a weightlifting machine circuit. I was determined to do at least as much weight as she did, although I was hoping to increase the amount (yes, an Identity issue). I was successful in my goal until we reached the rear deltoid machine. I was unable to move the handle at all at the weight she had been using. Plenty of sadness, shame and Identity loss as I was able to do only half the weight she had been using. Apparently, in my roles as a therapist and writer, I do not use my rear deltoid muscle very much, as they were terribly weak due to underuse.*

For most of us, our emotion processing 'muscle' has atrophied and is terribly weak due to underuse. We all did this really well early in life but lost the ability over time. This is why it is important to do the CEW every day, to reawaken and exercise that muscle.

People sometimes say they tried the Wheel but didn't keep doing it because it was difficult and too painful.

CONSIDER

Bowler Wannabe: Once I'm good at bowling, I'm going to start bowling. It's gonna be great whipping that ball down the lane and watching the pins fly as I hit strike after strike after strike! I'm so excited about getting good at it, so I can start bowling!

> *Friend: I think you're going to have to start bowling before you'll be good at it.*
>
> *Bowler Wannabe: What?! No way! I'm not going to start bowling before I'm good at it. That would be horrible. I'd look like an idiot throwing gutter balls and missing pins. I might even slip and fall; how humiliating would that be?! Also, they put your score up there so everyone can see it. People might make fun of me. I don't want people seeing me with a 58, especially with some little kid in the next lane with a 150 or something like that. Oh no (enacting bowling motion), I'm gonna start bowling once I'm really good at it.*
>
> *Friend: Hmmm . . . well, good luck with that.*
>
> *Bowler Wannabe: I won't need luck once I'm really good.*
>
> *Friend (nodding hesitantly): Riiiiiight.*

While the above scenario is silly, many of us often function this way relationally. We plan to implement the things that will help our relationships once we get good at them, when they're automatic and easy. The thought of attempting them before that time is intimidating and overwhelming, so we wait and wait and never quite begin what will bring success.

This is true for many people with the CEW. Some say it feels awkward, painful, forced, insincere, etc. This will be true for X number of times doing it, and we don't know what X is. So, hurry and get to X!

The Core Emotion Wheel is not the goal; it is a tool- a means to an end. The goal is being able to process emotion authentically as it happens in real time, which produces relational connection.

BRAIN (RE)TRAINING

The Core Emotion Wheel (CEW) experience retrains the participants' brains:

> *Retraining occurs as the sharer accesses core emotions, accurately identifies and verbalizes them in a manageable way.*
>
> *Retraining occurs as the other person experiences the sharer conveying emotion in a manageable way: from the core and in a position of vulnerability.*
>
> *Retraining occurs as the other person responds with an "Oooo," conveying 'presence' (with no defensiveness, arguing, explaining, fixing, etc). Escalation with its inherent damage does not occur, and de-escalation is not required.*
>
> *Retraining occurs as the sharer experiences safety.*
>
> *Retraining occurs after a successful CEW with a positive memory loop. As the number of successful CEWs increases, the loop becomes stronger, and the sharer becomes more prone to turn to the other.*

Many couples have been doing the Core Emotion Wheel experience every day for years; it is part of their daily routine: they brush their teeth every day; they do the Core Emotion Wheel every day. Some of these couples have a set time each day when they do the Wheel, and some set an alarm to remind them of this time.

Following are experiences couples have reported about doing the Wheel.

A couple was mad at each other after an unresolved conflict and had not spoken for hours. When his phone alarm went off for doing the Wheel, he got the Wheel, walked into the room where she was, threw the Wheel on the floor and announced, "It's time to do the stupid Wheel!" He then added, "And you're gonna have to go first, cause I need to Oooo you for a couple minutes."

When they shared the story of this experience, he said that, as he heard her convey her core emotions from a position of vulnerability and as he Ooooed her, he couldn't help feeling connection with her. He said he was mad, wanted to be mad and wanted to stay mad, but as he heard her core, he couldn't help feeling differently. Then, when he shared his half of the Wheel and she Ooooed him, he was moved even further until his whole perspective had changed. He reported being intrigued that he was not able to hold onto being mad at her.

He said, "I was kinda still mad at her, and I actually wanted to be mad at her, but I couldn't help being drawn to her." She reported a similar experience and that doing the Wheel drastically changed their trajectory for the evening.

Life consists of seconds, and this changed their life!

Ariana and (Dr) Blake (brand new Connection Coders):
Blake: The Core Emotion Wheel is stupid.
Therapist: Oooo, OK, what's happening with that?
Blake: Every day when I do it, I repeat the same thing, so it just sounds stupid.
Ariana (startled and turning to look at him): Oh Babe, what happens for you with that? What am I missing?
Blake: You were there- you saw it. I told you every day about my fear of losing my job or being sued or something.
Ariana: Mmmm ...
Therapist: So what happened for her when you did that?
Blake: I'm sure she thought it was stupid too.
Therapist: Can you ask her?
Blake: Ask her what?
Therapist: What happened for her when you repeated the same thing.
Blake (turning to his wife): What happened for you when I shared the same thing every day?
Ariana: Oh Babe, that was the most valuable thing for me this week, hearing about your fear.
Blake: Huh? What do you mean?
Therapist: Yes, what happened with that?
Ariana: Well, like we said last week, I thought he was just a butthead. (Blake had used the term "Butthead" to refer to himself the previous week, so it was safe for her to use it.) But this week I

realized that he gets hit with fear. His drive home from work is about twenty minutes, and he's experiencing fear that whole time. So, by the time he gets home, he's really struggling. But, this week, he just told me what was happening, and I got it.

Blake: Yeah, but I told you that every day. I figured you got sick of hearing it.

Ariana: Oh Babe, I loved it; so much joy.

Therapist: So, what am I missing here?

Ariana: Every day on the drive home, he plays through the day in his head. He evaluates and reevaluates what happened. Then he gets hit with fear that maybe he didn't handle everything right and that there could be problems.

Blake: As a doctor, I could be sued over something going wrong, and well, I guess this sounds dumb, but then I start thinking that we could lose everything and end up broke and homeless with our three kids.

(Therapist and Ariana both Oooo as Ariana reaches to hold Blake's hand.)

Therapist: Wow, that's a lot.

Ariana: Yeah, I get it Babe. That's a lot of pressure, and I get what happens that you need so much time to unwind when you get home.

Blake: It didn't seem as bad this week.

Ariana (grinning): Seemed like that to me too.

Therapist: So, you processed the emotion with your partner, and that changed it for you?

Blake: Yeah, except then I felt guilt for burdening her.
Therapist: Did she feel burdened?
Blake: Uh, I guess. I would imagine so.
Therapist: Can you ask her?
Blake: Ask her wh--oh right. Did you feel burdened by me sharing my fear?
Ariana (grinning again): Oh Babe, not at all. I felt so much joy that you would turn to me and share with me. I did feel sad that this messes with you so much, but I want you to always share with me!
Blake: The same thing every day?!
Ariana: If that's what's happening for you, yes.
Blake (with a slight smile): OK

Glenn:

A couple sat in my office during our fourth session together. During each of our previous sessions, she had done the Core Emotion Wheel experience smoothly. He had not been able to do it at all but instead sat staring blankly at it for long periods. In such settings, a minute feels much longer than sixty seconds, and several minutes of silence are painful.

As the time dragged on and we waited for something, anything to emit from him, I stared at the paper in my notebook, doodled, counted my heartbeats, contemplated whether I had hydrated adequately, thought of Phyllis and the beach and waited. As my blood pressure dipped and I feared it was approaching 0/0, I suddenly burst out, "You know what, Dude? Just make up stuff." (This was not my finest moment as a therapist. My response was out of impatience, exasperation, even desperation. Nonetheless, what ensued was remarkable!)

Male partner: Huh?

Glenn: Just make up stuff.

Male partner (befuddled): What do you mean?

Glenn (turning to female partner): Could you Oooo him if he made up stuff?

Female partner (laughing lightly): I guess so.

Glenn (turning back to male partner): Just say to her something like, "I felt fear last week when I was kidnapped by that drug cartel."

Glenn (turning to female partner): Could you Oooo him if he said that to you?

Female partner (laughing again): Yeah, I could do that.

He then quite smoothly conveyed the following:

"I felt lonely that you didn't come to this appointment with me."

"I felt guilt that I ate all the food in our house and left you to go hungry all week."

"I felt sad that you had a sex change last week."

"I felt joy that we won the lottery this morning."

"I felt fear last week when you drove our car off a cliff with us in it."

"I felt anger about that too."

> *"I felt shame when you made me go to the store naked."*
> *"I felt hurt by that too."*
>
> In our first three sessions, they sat on the couch as far apart as possible. As he shared his core emotions, she Ooooed him and then physically moved towards him. Despite the fact that she knew he was making up the scenarios associated with the core emotions, she nonetheless moved towards him! She was moved by his sharing, even though she knew the scenarios were not real.

While it is not the goal to present untrue or unreal scenarios, if we can get to the core emotions from a place of vulnerability, human connection is facilitated.

CORE EMOTION WHEEL EXPERIENCE - ISSUE SPECIFIC

An issue specific Core Emotion Wheel guides through processing emotions concerning a particular situation. It helps to put a label on it, such as "Buying a new car." Processing the emotions surrounding the issue assists you to think clearly and make a better decision, as well as not disconnecting with each other over it.

The procedure is the same as for the daily Core Emotion Wheel experience, at the core, from a position of vulnerability, lots of Ooooing, except that each emotion pertains to the specifically labeled issue. You will not always have all eight emotions about every issue but, most usually will apply.

STUNT DOUBLE

Humans connect through core emotion presented authentically from a position of vulnerability. This is how we are born; this is how we are coded. As young children, we are authentic and vulnerable; we do not know how to be otherwise. Over time we get reprogrammed (but never recoded) to be *in*authentic. The Connection Codes are helping people around the world gain authenticity, leading to deep connection.

However, there is an important caveat: at times it is appropriate and better to be *in*authentic. This is important to note, because there are settings where inauthenticity is better than authenticity. Deep relational connection cannot develop with inauthenticity, but it is important to cover this exception.

In Hollywood, when a scene is especially dangerous or vulnerable, a stunt double may step in to protect the actor. The stunt double appears to be the actor but actually is not. And people want to connect with the authentic actor, not the stunt double.

In the same way, each of us has a stunt double. When a scenario seems especially dangerous or vulnerable, our stunt double may step in to protect us. Our stunt double appears to be us but actually is not. And others want to connect with our authentic selves not our stunt doubles.

A 14-year-old boy who enjoys playing with Legos may experience harm in authentically revealing that information to an unsafe, unkind person. The unkind person is wrong for their unkindness. Nonetheless, it might be better not to share authentically. The 14-year-old's stunt double may need to step in to protect him.

There are also scenarios where a stunt double is needed to protect another person.

CUT OFF THE TALL

Glenn:

Our oldest child Echo (co-author of this book) was quite precocious and learned to speak fluently quite early. When she was two, she and I were standing in line at the post office to get stamps (back when you stood in line at the post office to get stamps).

Echo (suddenly exclaiming in wonderment as she stared wide-eyed behind me): Daddy, look how fat that man is!

Me (whispering, flooded with embarrassment and panic): Echo, don't say that.

Echo (excited and persistent): Daddy, you have to look. He's so fat.

Me (aware of someone standing behind them): Echo, stop saying that.

Echo (undeterred and emphatic): Daddy, just look. He's so fat!

Me (whispering louder and more emphatically): I'm not going to look, and stop saying that right now!

Echo (pleading): Daddy, I just want you to look at him. He really is so fat!

Me (squatting beside the sub-four footer): Echo, I am not going to look, and you are not to say that again. Do you understand?!

Echo (with tears forming in her eyes): Daddy, I just wanted you to see how--

Me (perplexed): I know, and we'll talk about it when we get in the car.

> We waited in line, with me trying to shield the person behind us from my daughter's stare, while she continuously attempted to catch another glance of this fascinating marvel. We got our stamps and exited to our car.
>
> Echo: Daddy, why wouldn't you look at that man? I wanted you to see him. He's really fat!
>
> Me: Yes, I know, but we don't call people fat.
>
> Echo: But he is fat, really fat. He's the fattest person...
>
> Me: Yes, I know, but we don't call people fat.
>
> Echo: But Daddy, he is --
>
> Me: Echo, there are some things we don't say, because it can really hurt someone's feelings.
>
> Echo (concerned and bewildered): Daddy, I wasn't trying to hurt his feelings. I just wanted you to look at how fat he is.
>
> Me (realizing this two-year-old was not going to be able to grasp this social construct): I know, but there are some things we just don't say, and we don't say fat. We might say someone is tall, but we don't say fat. Do you understand?
>
> Echo (staring blankly for a moment): But Daddy, he wasn't tall, he was fat.
>
> Me (resolved that she just wasn't going to get it yet): Ok, but we're not going to say fat.
>
> Echo: Ok Daddy, (then adding quietly) but he was really fat.

> We got home and went to the kitchen where Phyllis was fixing dinner.
> Echo: Hi Mommy, what are you doing?
> Phyllis: I'm fixing dinner.
> Echo: Can I help you? What are you doing now?
> Phyllis: Cutting the fat off the chicken.
> Echo (gasping and appalled): Mommy, we do not say fat!! We say tall!
> For years in our household, we cut off the tall, not the fat.

Echo did not have a stunt double; she did not know how to be inauthentic and thus appropriate.

OTHER EXAMPLES

Husband to wife as she stares at the little stick thing: *You're pregnant?!?! How the heck did that happen?! I'm flooded with fear!*

Wedding attendee: *What a bummer that this is all you're serving at your reception. I thought we'd be having a sit down dinner, not those stale mint things.*

Friend: *I feel joy that you also think that dress makes you look fat.*

Husband (between his wife's contractions): *I felt hurt that you yelled at me about getting you more ice.*

Starting business meeting: *Hello everyone and welcome. I want to be transparent here. I'm totally unprepared for today's business negotiation and fairly inept as well.*

Quarterback in first huddle of Super Bowl: *I'm terrified! They are so much better than us. We're about to get destroyed! We don't stand a chance!!*

NOT *HERE!*

Glenn:

I was sitting with an unemployed young man, discussing his job prospects. He explained how his interviews would go, "*I'm always authentic with them- I know how much you stress authenticity. When they ask where I see myself in five years, I tell them, 'Not here!'*"

He needed a stunt double.

There are times when inauthenticity is appropriate and better. Nonetheless, we will not be able to connect deeply without authenticity. Some of us are continuously in stunt double mode. In some relationships, both parties are continuously in stunt double mode. Some of us have been in stunt double mode so continuously for so long that we don't even realize it, and we don't know how to be authentic. It may take some time and great effort to recognize this so as to get to authenticity and connection.

SECTION 3 TAKEAWAYS

Do the Core Emotion Wheel every day.

Do an issue specific Core Emotion Wheel.

Strive to implement processing emotions in the moment.

CORE EMOTION WHEEL
EXPERIENCE EXAMPLE 1

I feel anger with negative assumptions about me.

I feel fear when I submit an essay for publication.

I feel guilt when I treat people unkindly.

I feel shame when I don't meet the expectations of friends or family.

I feel loneliness when I am misunderstood.

I feel sadness when a loved one passes away.

I feel hurt when I ask a friend to spend time with me and they don't show up.

I feel joy when I see my children protect each other or learn something new.

CORE EMOTION WHEEL
EXPERIENCE EXAMPLE 2

I feel anger when people say unkind things about me.

I feel fear when I miss a deadline at work.

I feel guilt when I miss my kids' ball games.

I feel shame when my spouse expresses disappointment about me.

I feel loneliness when my friends hang out and don't invite me.

I feel sadness when I see a loved one hurting.

I feel hurt when my spouse answers the phone while I am talking to them.

I feel joy when I am on a road trip with my family.

CORE EMOTION WHEEL
EXPERIENCE EXAMPLE 3

I feel anger when you get stuck or lost in our conflict.

I feel so lonely when we are in conflict. You are my best friend.

I felt sad when we were stuck in our tension.

I felt guilt for bringing up our conflict with friends before talking to you about it.

I feel fear when we get stuck and the Connection Codes don't seem to be working.

I feel shame when you correct me on my word usage.

I felt so much joy when you sent me the text that said, "Love you tons. So sorry I get lost." Such a balm, I just melt.

CORE EMOTION WHEEL
EXPERIENCE EXAMPLE 4

I feel lonely when you don't tune into what I am saying.

Sometimes I feel hurt by that too.

And then sometimes I feel anger, mostly secondary from the hurt.

I feel guilt when I overreact and make things worse between us.

I feel shame sometimes when you tease me about things, especially in front of our friends.

I feel fear that our friends will think poorly of me and won't like me.

I felt sad that there was tension between us the other day when that happened.

I feel a lot of joy that you were able to hear me and that we were able to reconnect.

CORE EMOTION WHEEL - ISSUE SPECIFIC EXPERIENCE

EXAMPLE 1: BUYING A NEW CAR

Fred:

I feel joy about buying this car; it's been my dream car since I was a teenager.

I feel fear because I'm not sure we can afford it.

I feel guilt spending so much money on something that's not mandatory. I could keep driving my old unreliable car.

I feel shame that it feels so Identity bringing to me; I love the image of me in this new car. I don't like the image of me in my old car.

I feel lonely, a little bit unpartnered, cause I don't see excitement from you about this new car.

I feel sad that we've driven crappy unreliable cars, with no air conditioning for most of our lives.

I feel anger about that too.

I feel hurt that my brother told me it was stupid to buy a new car.

Wilma:

I feel sad that it's such a struggle for you to spend the money for this car.

I feel fear too that it's too expensive and also some fear that people will judge you for buying a new car.

I feel lonely that it seems like you've left me out of your dream of owning this car.

I feel guilt about that too, that I haven't felt safe for you to share that with me.

I also feel hurt about that; I want you to share all of you with me. I want to matter to you that much and be totally safe for you.

I feel joy about you having this car. I think you deserve it!

I feel anger that your brother said that to you.

I don't really feel any shame about this.

EXAMPLE 2: HAVING ANOTHER BABY

Sharon:

I feel sad about pausing our adventures and activities to go through the two year whirlwind of having another baby. But, I also feel sad about never again experiencing pregnancy, breastfeeding or having a new baby.

I feel loneliness with how much of the responsibility of having a baby falls on me.

I feel hurt about the disconnection we experienced when we had our last baby.

And I guess I feel fear that will happen again; yeah, some fear that our marriage will suffer, my mental and/or physical health will suffer and the baby won't be safe and healthy.

I feel shame about gaining weight and having my body change again.

I feel guilt that gaining weight is a factor for this decision.

I don't think I feel any anger about this.

I feel 43 feet of joy to meet and snuggle and live life with another little person.

Aaron:

I feel fear about providing for a bigger family. I also feel fear about the pregnancy and infancy.

I feel loneliness about sharing you with another person.

There is sadness in that too.

I feel guilt that so much of the responsibilities with our babies falls on you.

I guess there is shame in that too.

I feel anger that I have any hesitancy in this at all.

I feel a lot of joy about our family and getting to share it with another person.

I don't feel any hurt about this.

STUNT DOUBLE EXPERIENCE ASSIGNMENT

My stunt double shows up when

My stunt double shows up with *you* when

I experience *your* stunt double when

I'm always a stunt double with (a person in your life), because

STUNT DOUBLE EXPERIENCE EXAMPLE 1

My stunt double shows up when someone questions me about a proposal at work, and I feel inadequate.

My stunt double shows up with you when you ask about our finances.

I experience your stunt double when you feel hurt by something I've said, but you respond sarcastically.

I'm always a stunt double with my mom, because I don't feel comfortable being vulnerable with her. She usually belittles my concerns.

STUNT DOUBLE EXPERIENCE EXAMPLE 2

My stunt double shows up when I feel uncomfortable with someone, so I get obnoxious.

My stunt double shows up with you when you say something about my weight and I feel hurt, but I tell you to mind your own business.

I experience your stunt double when I criticize your parenting style, and you say you know a lot more than me about being a good parent.

I'm always a stunt double with my boss, because he criticizes me so harshly. I lose so much identity with him, because he treats me like I'm stupid.

Doing the Core Emotion Wheel every day facilitates the ability of conveying authentically in real time, in the moment. This can be an incremental development, and utilizing the four phrases facilitates this. This is laid out in the following:

CORE EMOTION WHEEL - 4 INCREMENTS EXPERIENCE

1ST INCREMENT:

Sharer: I feel _____

Partner: Oooo (or some version).

2ND INCREMENT:

Sharer: I feel _____

Partner: Oooo, what happens for you there? What am I missing?

Sharer: I feel _____

_____

Partner: Oooo.

3RD INCREMENT:

Sharer: I feel _____

Partner: Oooo, what happens for you there? What am I missing?

Sharer: I feel _____
_____

Partner: Oooo, how can I help with that?

Sharer: _____
_____

Partner: Oooo.

4TH INCREMENT:

Sharer: I feel _____

Partner: Oooo, what happens for you there? What am I missing?

Sharer: I feel _____
_____

Partner: Oooo, how can I help with that?

Sharer: _____
_____

Partner (becomes the sharer as roles switch): Oooo, when I hear that I feel _____

Original sharer (now the partner): Oooo.

CORE EMOTION WHEEL – 4 INCREMENTS EXPERIENCE EXAMPLE

1ST INCREMENT:

Sharer: I feel fear about our finances.

Partner: Oooo.

2ND INCREMENT:

Sharer: I feel fear about our finances.

Partner: Oooo, what happens for you there? What am I missing?

Sharer: I feel fear cause I don't know where our money goes; seems like we're not really spending wisely, you know, making the most of our hard-earned money.

Partner: Mmmm, yeah.

3RD INCREMENT:

Sharer: I feel fear about our finances.

Partner: Oooo, what happens for you there? What am I missing?

Sharer: I feel fear cause I don't know where our money goes; seems like we're not really spending wisely, you know, making the most of our hard-earned money.

Partner: Mmmm, yeah. How can I help with that?

Sharer: I think maybe having a budget that we kept would help.

Partner: Yeah, ok.

4TH INCREMENT:

Sharer: I feel fear about our finances.

Partner: Oooo, what happens for you there? What am I missing?

Sharer: I feel fear cause I don't know where our money goes; seems like we're not really spending wisely, you know, making the most of our hard-earned money.

Partner: Mmmm, yeah. How can I help with that?

Sharer: I think us having a budget that we kept together would help.

Partner: Yeah, ok. (roles switch) Ugh, I feel shame when I hear that.

Original sharer: Oooo, what happens with shame for you? I missed that.

Current (new) sharer: I feel shame that I haven't already created a budget.

Partner: Oh ok. How can I help with that?

Sharer: Maybe remind me that we'll do it together, for us, for our family.

Partner: Oooo, yeah I can definitely do that. I feel joy when I hear that from you.

Section 3
Focus

Do the Core Emotion Wheel every day.

SECTION 4

The Cycle

Every relationship has a cycle, which is what happens when people interact. One person says or does something; the other responds, the first person responds to that response, etc.

CONSIDER

You and a friend are walking through a park when you notice a few leaves and a paper towel swirling around. The two of you watch as a whirlwind spins and moves across a field onto a playground. You continue to watch, when abruptly the leaves stop moving, the paper towel falls to the ground and the whirlwind disappears.

A whirlwind is entertaining and causes no damage or fear. The same process happening with a whirlwind is happening with a cyclone. Air is moving in a circle, except on a much faster and bigger scale. However, a cyclone is not entertaining and causes terrible damage and fear.

Every relationship has a cycle; every interaction has a cycle. Damage occurs when the cycle escalates and becomes a cyclone. When a relational cycle increases in speed and size, the damage that occurs takes a lot of time and effort to repair.

No cyclone lasts forever. The swirling air escalates but eventually will deescalate and stop. The problem is all the damage that occurs when the cycle escalates. In the same way, no relational cyclone lasts forever. The interaction escalates but eventually will deescalate and stop. The problem is the damage that occurs when the cycle escalates. No one high fives after a tornado leaves the neighborhood. No one proclaims, "Yay, we won! The tornado's gone!" If they did, the response would be, "Yeah, but look at your home. It's going to take a year to rebuild what the tornado destroyed in a few minutes!" The same is true with relational cyclones. It can take years to rebuild what the cyclone destroyed in a few minutes.

The *cyclone* is what causes the damage; the *cyclone* is the enemy. This mentality helps us remember we're partners on the same team in preventing cyclones. Also, most people panic when a tornado is coming. No one says, "Hey, let's go beat up that tornado!" Once the cycle escalates and gets faster and bigger, the relationship is already being damaged.

SLOWER IS FASTER

Because of the destructive nature of the disconnect that results from relational cyclones, the speed and size of our cycles must be limited. Each of us has had interactions that escalated to cyclone level and horribly damaged the relationship. The pain and exhaustion last long after deescalation. If the cycle doesn't become a cyclone, extra time and energy are not expended repairing and recovering.

The goal is to operate in *pre*escalation, avoiding the harm of the cyclone. The four phrases (Oooo. What's happening? I missed it. How can I help?) are powerful in keeping a cycle slow and small, preventing cyclones. The four phrases make safe space for emotion to be processed, preventing escalation. Therefore, deescalation is not needed, and the relationship is not damaged.

So, for interactions, slower is faster, smaller is better. When we keep the relational cycles slow and small, we can process what's happening and remain connected. Tense interactions no longer last for hours or days but only minutes or seconds.

> *When the cycle gets faster,*
> *it leads to disaster!*

Phyllis:
In our first 20 years of marriage, Glenn and I had countless cyclones. They were triggered by certain topics and so predictable- clearly our cycle. The main triggering topics were my family of origin and sex (or the lack of). Those conversations never went well. They always led to cyclones and caused so much pain. We desperately needed an extra large box of Oooos.

Now we use the four phrases continually, and our cycle virtually never escalates. Because of this we rarely ever disconnect, literally only a few times a year. I am so thankful for this, as well as surprised. Living in deep connection, without cyclones, is wonderfully peaceful. Life can be so beautiful!

No Cyclone Zone!

FEEL SMALL, GET BIG!!
(IT'S TOUGH TO HUG A WOLF)

When we feel threatened, the brain signals, "Danger!" This is not intentional; it is instinctual. The brain is not *trying* to signal danger- it is brain chemistry. When the brain signals danger, the involuntary automatic response is fight, flight or freeze (the 3 Fs). This response is not bad or wrong; this response is human.

If we're walking through a forest and encounter a wolf, fear activates in the brain in response to the perceived threat and signals, "Danger!" When we feel threatened, we feel 'small' and must get 'big' to increase power to manage the threat and protect ourselves. Anger activates in the brain, because anger is the best way to get 'big,' to increase power. Again, we do not try to do any of this; it is involuntary and automatic- it is human.

Fear gets our attention, and anger motivates us to action. We do not hug the wolf; we just try to survive the wolf. We must quickly determine which of the 3 Fs provides the best chance for survival.

Fight? Are we big enough to fight the wolf and win? Do we have something that will make us bigger or stronger: a gun, a stick, a club, a scream, etc.?

Flight? Are we fast enough to outrun the wolf? Is there something that will make us faster? Can we climb a tree to escape the wolf?

Freeze? Can we be still enough that the wolf will not notice us- maybe play dead? Is there something that will distract the wolf or hide us from its view?

In relationships, when we feel threatened, the brain signals, "Danger!" This is not intentional; it is instinctual. The brain is not *trying* to signal danger- it is brain chemistry. When the brain signals danger, the involuntary automatic response is fight, flight or freeze (the 3 Fs). This response is not bad or wrong; this response is human.

A relational cyclone is a stressor and a threat, which we reference as a 'wolf.' If we're walking through life and encounter a 'wolf', fear activates in the brain in response to the perceived threat and signals, "Danger!" When we feel threatened, we feel 'small' and must get 'big' to increase power to manage the threat and protect ourselves. Anger activates in the brain, because anger is the best way to get 'big,' to increase power. Again, we do not try to do any of this; it is involuntary and automatic- it is human.

Fear gets our attention, and anger motivates us to action. We do not consider hugging the wolf; we only consider surviving the wolf. We must quickly determine which of the 3 Fs provides the best chance for survival.

Two problems: 1) Anger increases the speed and size of relational cycles and turns them into cyclones. 2) In the forest with an actual wolf, the three Fs protect you and can save your life. In relationships, all three Fs are loses.

Fight? Fighting damages the relationship, so you lose.
Flight? Fleeing damages the relationship, so you lose.
Freeze? Freezing damages the relationship, so you lose.

Each of us can appear like a threat or a 'wolf' to another. This is not a judgement, indictment or accusation. This may have nothing to do with you, even if it's all about you- this is about what happens for the other. Each of us can be unkind, which will feel wolfish to another, but someone can experience us as a wolf even when our intention and behavior is good.

As the other encounters a wolf, fear and anger activate in the brain and the fight/flight/freeze instinct kicks in. This increases the relational cycle's speed and size and the interaction escalates. At some point it will deescalate, but damage will have been done and the relationship will require repair. Thus, the goal is to partner against the threat of the wolf. Identifying and verbalizing the appearance of the wolf followed by Ooooing creates this partnership.

Echo:
We can experience a total stranger as a wolf. When I was eight months pregnant with our last baby, I was taking a walk through some farmland near our house. A windowless van passed me multiple times, and I was hit with fear. The driver probably was lost, but I felt fear that he had turned around to kidnap me.

This had nothing to do with him, even though it was all about him. This was about what happened inside of me. He did nothing wrong. He might not have noticed me, but for that moment, he had become a wolf to me.

Nothing happened. We did not interact at all, but I was flooded with fear from the perceived threat from a completely innocent person. He had become a wolf to me, not because he was bad, but because of what was happening in my brain.

CONSIDER

Someone shows you a picture of a wolf. You comment on the appearance of the magnificent creature: It's fur is spectacular with elaborate coloration. It's stature is massive with obvious power, and its fangs are huge and threatening. You both conclude it must be the Alpha of the pack, as surely none other could compete.

You comment, "Wow, that is a breathtaking sight. I would love to see such an extraordinary creature in real life!"

Your companion responds, "Oh, OK," as they open the door and let that very same wolf into the room.

Suddenly, your entire perspective changes; your admiration is completely overshadowed by the fear of that same canine!

It's tough to hug a wolf!

When a wolf appears, we feel threatened and the brain signals danger. It does not matter who the wolf is, the brain signals danger! It does not matter if it's a wonderful spouse, loving parent, favorite sibling, lifelong friend, kind neighbor, friendly clerk or the world's greatest boss. The experience is the same, and it's tough to hug a wolf!

WASPS & MOSQUITOS

Often the intensity of an interactional experience may seem less than a 'Wolf,' and Connection Coders sometimes reference this as wasps or mosquitos. A wasp sting is intense but typically less life threatening than a Wolf. A mosquito bite often is not noticed immediately and is typically less harmful than a Wasp or Wolf, but nonetheless produces pain.

Example:

Jose: Ow, I just got stung by a wasp!

Chante: Oooo, wow, should I get the bug spray.

Jose: No, it was an internal wasp.

Chante: Oooo, what happened? What's the wasp? What did I miss?

Jose: Hurt- I felt hurt by what you said.

Chante: Oh my, so what happened? I missed it.

Jose: Well, you said something about your dad being much farther along in his career by the time he was my age. Oooo, and there's some shame too.

Chante: Oh wow, yeah I get that. That stinks. How can I help with that?

UNSPOKEN WORDS

In interactions, all of us experience words, phrases and sentences that the other person did not say. We do not try to do this and often are unaware it is happening. Also, the speaker may not think, feel, know or believe the content of the message that was received. Frequently the message received is very far from the speaker's intent. Nonetheless, we clearly 'hear' these unspoken messages, and they can greatly affect interactions and relational connection.

Examples (unspoken words in parentheses):

You liked that movie?! (Wow, you have bad taste.)

Why did you do that? (You moron.)

How many cookies have you eaten? (You are fat, and you eat too much.)

So, what did you do today? (Obviously not much because the house is a mess.)

So. you didn't finish your degree? (Uneducated loser.)

It's important to us to live in a diverse neighborhood. (We are better than you, since you don't.)

All of our children are adopted because why have biological children when there are already so many who need a family? (Shame on you for having so many biological children and not adopting any children.)

Are you wearing that to the wedding? (It looks like a house dress.)

What time did you get up this morning? (Lazy sluggard.)

What time did you go to bed last night? (When will you get your act together?!)

> Wow, you did laundry; thank you! (You finally did something useful.)
>
> I had lunch with Sally yesterday. (I prefer time with her, not you.)
>
> You spent how much on groceries? (You suck at budgeting.)
>
> After three kids, I still weigh what I weighed on my wedding day. (And you should too, Fatso.)
>
> I got up at 5:00 and went for a run this morning! (You should stop being lazy and get up to run too.)

Example:
> Her: Babe, did you send that email?
>
> What he heard: You haven't sent that email yet?! Why not?! You are incompetent and unproductive. I am shocked at how incapable you are. I get sick of you not following through and doing what you were supposed to do. You always do this!!

She did not say any of that. She may not even have thought any of it. Nevertheless, he experienced it.

How to partner against the wolf:
> Her: Babe, did you send that email?
>
> Him: Oooo, that felt kinda wolfish.
>
> Her: Oooo, wow, that stinks. What happened? I missed it.
>
> Him: Kinda felt like you were saying I'm incompetent and unproductive and that you're shocked at what a pitiful person I am.

Her: Oh wow, that's intense. Yeah, that's a lot.
Him: Yeah, I lost Identity when you said that; I feel bad about myself. And no, I didn't get the email sent yet. Feels kinda overwhelming.
Her: Oooo, wow, that's a lot. How can I help?
Him: I'm not sure. Well, actually I could probably write it right now while we're sitting here. Could I run it by you in a couple of minutes?
Her: Sure, that'd be great.

This is how Connection Coders around the world are partnering against the wolf, keeping cycles from becoming cyclones, avoiding disconnection and winning in their interactions and relationships!

CONSIDER

I did not say he stole the car.

I *did not say he stole the car.*   *Someone said it, but it was not me.*

*I did **not** say he stole the car.*   *I flatly deny having said that.*

*I did not **say** he stole the car.*   *I thought it, but I didn't actually say it.*

*I did not say **he** stole the car.*   *I said someone stole it; I didn't say he did.*

*I did not say he **stole** the car.*   *I said he took it but
                                         not that he stole it.*

*I did not say he stole **the** car.*   *He stole a car but
                                         not the one in question.*

*I did not say he stole the **car**.*   *He stole the boat
                                         not the car.*

Only eight words but seven distinctly different meanings influenced by inflection, tone, presentation, previous interactions and experiences, the hearer's perspective, etc. So many variables affect our communication and thus our connection.

> *I know you believe you understand what you think I said, but I am not sure you realize that what you heard is not what I meant.*

Phyllis:

Over the years, as Glenn became safer with me, he developed a practice where he says, "You will not believe what my wife said to me today" or "Guess what my wife said to me today." I'll respond with, "Oooo, what happened? What did I miss? What did she say?"

He then tells me the things he experienced me saying- the unspoken words, phrases and sentences, many of which are awful.

I'll respond with something like: "Oooo, that's intense; that's a lot."

I did not say, think, feel or believe those things, but I get that he experienced them. And we both know he was not trying to hear them; he just did. There is no escalation with our cycle, and it lasts less than a minute.

Often the wolf appears when the other person hears unspoken words, phrases and sentences and experiences a threat.

PERCEPTION IS REALITY

What do you see in these pictures? Different people see different things, and it is not a question of who is right or wrong. For a variety of reasons, one person sees one thing while another person sees something very different. The individual is not *trying* to see a particular picture and may not be able to see a different picture even if coached.

Extensive research tells us that a number of people witnessing an occurrence may report that same number of variations on what occurred. Only one event occurred, but there are myriad factors that affect what a person experiences and remembers.

This is equally true in relational interactions. The experience of one can be very different from that of another. Neither person is *trying* to experience the event or interaction a particular way; they simply do. The other is not *trying* to hear a particular message; they simply do.

> *When the reaction to the situation seems unwarranted, someone has left the building (or at least is no longer present).*

DELETE "MAKES ME"

In attempting to lessen unspoken words, phrases and sentences along with their damaging effect, we have found that eliminating the phrase "makes me" is a great benefit.

Examples:
You make me sad when you do that.
You made me mad earlier.
That makes me feel shame.
It makes me feel hurt when you say that.

The phrase "makes me" is an accusation and hinders

connection. It complicates interaction, as we now have to determine whether the other *made* us feel an emotion or if we simply felt it. It distracts from processing emotion, delaying or even stopping the process. Simply presenting the core emotion and skipping the "makes me" simplifies the interaction. Also, usually it is not possible to prove or disprove that someone *made* us feel something or if the emotion simply happened. Additionally, it doesn't really matter. Humans connect through emotion, not the logistics of where the emotion originated.

APOLOGIES

Apologizing rarely leads to connection. Apologies frequently are used as a defense mechanism or even a weapon. For example:
> "Oh, sorry. That's not what I meant by that."
> "I'm sorry. I didn't know that would bother you."
> "OK, OK, I'm sorry. You don't have to make such a big deal about it!"
> "I'm sorry. I'm sorry! What do you want- blood?!"
> "I said I'm sorry. You just need to forgive and stop holding such a grudge."

Conveying the core emotion connects. For example:
> "Oooo, I feel guilt about what I said. I really missed on that- so crappy. You're really important to me, and it brought you pain. Guilt, guilt, guilt. What else happens for you there?"

There has been no apology, but this connects.

> *Apologies are free (but you probably don't need one).*

TRAJECTORY

When aiming at a target, heading in a direction or striving toward a goal, a slight alteration at the beginning can greatly affect whether we achieve the desired result. This is because of trajectory- the end is affected significantly by the beginning. The same is true with interactions; a slight alteration at the beginning can greatly affect whether we achieve the desired result. What happens in the first ten seconds of an interaction can greatly affect what happens over the next ten hours or even longer.

When we follow the energy, we keep cycles from escalating. This changes the trajectory of interactions and affects what happens in the coming seconds, minutes, hours and days. Following the energy makes safe space for the other person to process emotion. Whenever there is relational disconnection, it is important to go back to the first unprocessed emotion and process it. Unprocessed emotion disconnects; processed emotion connects!

SECTION 4 TAKEAWAYS

Every interaction has a cycle; the goal is to keep it from becoming a cyclone.

The cyclone is the enemy, not you or the other person.

Slower is faster: when the cycle gets faster, it leads to disaster. No cyclone zone!

When we feel small, we get big.

It's tough to hug a Wolf. Each of us can look like a wolf.

In relationships, all 3 Fs are loses.

The threat of the wolf is the enemy, not you or the other.

We experience unspoken words, phrases and sentences.

Perception is reality.

Changing our trajectory can change the world!

THE CYCLE EXPERIENCE ASSIGNMENT

I would describe our cyclone as

An example of a time intense emotion shut down my cognition:

An example of a time I experienced unspoken words, phrases and sentences:

When there is a wolf, my reaction most likely is:

>   *fight*   *flight*   *freeze*

When I experience you as a wolf, my reaction most likely is:

>   *fight*   *flight*   *freeze*

When I feel small, I protect myself by

When I feel small with *you*, I protect myself by

I become a wolf when

I experience *you* as a wolf when

An example of a time when following the energy changed the trajectory:

THE CYCLE EXPERIENCE EXAMPLE

I would describe our cycle as an uncontrolled wildfire.

An example of a time intense emotion shut down my cognition: When I leave work late at night, I get hit with fear and end up running to my car.

An example of a time I experienced unspoken words, phrases and sentences: When my mother asks me if I remembered to fill the car with gas.

When there is a wolf, my reaction most likely is:

    fight   **_flight_**   *freeze*

When I experience you as a wolf, my reaction most likely is:

    fight   *flight*   **_freeze_**

When I feel small, I protect myself by talking faster and louder.

When I feel small with *you*, I protect myself by threatening to leave you.

I become a wolf when someone is making fun of me.

I experience *you* as a wolf when you correct my word usage.

An example of a time when following the energy changed the trajectory: When my son said he lost his job, instead of lecturing, I asked what happened. I heard his heart. I expressed my fear, he Ooooed me and we connected.

Section 4
Focus

Be aware of your cycle this week. Remember that the Cyclone and the Wolf are the enemy, not you or the other person. Oooo and follow the energy to keep cycles slow and small and partner against the threat.

SECTION 5
Relationship Science

Stressors are part of the human condition and experience- they always have been and always will be. They look differently in various settings, but every human experiences stressors. That is a reality that will not change.

In the 1960s, psychiatrists Thomas Holmes and Richard Rahe conducted extensive research regarding whether stress contributes to illness. They developed The Social Readjustment Rating Scale, commonly referenced as the Holmes-Rahe scale (see next page), which ranks the intensity of life stressors from one to 100 points. Their research indicated that the higher someone scored on the scale, the more likely they were to become ill, particularly if they surpassed 300 points.

HOLMES-RAHE SCALE[1]

1. Death of spouse (100)
2. Divorce (73)
3. Marital separation (65)
4. Jail term (63)
5. Death of close family member (63)
6. Personal injury or illness (53)
7. Marriage (50)
8. Fired at work (47)
9. Marital reconciliation (45)
10. Retirement (45)
11. Change in health of family member (44)
12. Pregnancy (40)
13. Sex difficulties (39)
14. Gain of new family member (39)
15. Business readjustment (39)
16. Change in financial state (38)
17. Death of close friend (37)
18. Change to a different line of work (36)
19. Change in number of arguments with spouse (35)
20. A large mortgage or loan (31)
21. Foreclosure of mortgage or loan (30)
22. Change in responsibilities at work (29)
23. Son or daughter leaving home (29)
24. Trouble with in-laws (29)
25. Outstanding personal achievement (28)

1 Holmes, T. H., & Rahe, R. H. (1967). The Social Readjustment Rating Scale. *Journal of Psychosomatic Research, 11*(2), 213–218. Doi:10.1016/0022-3999(67)90010-4

26. Spouse begins or stops work (26)
27. Begin or end school/college (26)
28. Change in living conditions (25)
29. Revision of personal habits (24)
30. Trouble with boss (23)
31. Change in work hours or conditions (20)
32. Change in residence (20)
33. Change in school/college (20)
34. Change in recreation (19)
35. Change in church activities (19)
36. Change in social activities (18)
37. A moderate loan or mortgage (17)
38. Change in sleeping habits (16)
39. Change in number of family get-togethers (15)
40. Change in eating habits (15)
41. Vacation (13)
42. Christmas (12)
43. Minor violations of the law (11)

Stressors are a part of life- that will not change. What *can* change is the teamship in which stressors are managed. Handling stressors with others with whom you are connected is a completely different experience than handling stressors alone. The effects of this are distinctly and vastly different as well! This is what we reference as Relationship Science.

PSYCHOLATION

Humans are the least likely species on the planet to survive independently but the most likely to thrive *inter*dependently. We are born needing relational connection to thrive, even to survive. That does not change as we age. We develop and maintain interdependence through emotional connection, which facilitates us becoming the best versions of ourselves- successful and powerful.

Every human *deserves* to live in deep connection and to experience the safety and joy that such deep connection brings. Relational connection is the essence of life. That alone is reason enough to implement the Connection Codes on the journey of life. However, a mounting body of evidence is shedding light on the extensive effects, both positive and negative, of relationships and emotion on the human experience.

The negative consequences of *not* living connected is so significant, it deserves addressing. The antithesis of deep connection is psychological isolation or psycholation. Psycholation is isolation of the psyche, where authenticity does not occur and what is happening at the core is not conveyed and processed. An individual can live in psycholation, as can a couple, family, group, church, business or community.

Extensive research is revealing the damaging effect of psycholation; a mounting body of evidence indicates many debilitating illnesses, including cancers, are facilitated by unprocessed emotion. When we do not live in connection, we do not process emotion; processing emotion facilitates connection.

An oversimplified note on cancer: If someone hands you a pen and you hand it back to them and they hand it back to you and you hand it back to them and you continue to repeat this, at some point you will drop the pen. The two of you might complete this simple process many times, but at some point, you will drop the pen. If you repeat any process enough times, at some point there will be a mistake.

There are trillions of cells in the human body. These cells are continuously replicating themselves. This process is far more complex than handing a pen back and forth. At some point, that replication process is going to be incorrect, there will be a mistake resulting in a faulty cancerous cell.

Many cancerous cells are not viable, so there is no threat to the body. Also, cells contain coding to self-destruct when they are not properly functional, a process called apoptosis. For unknown reasons, some cancerous cells ignore the message of that coding and do not self-destruct. Nonetheless, one cancerous cell out of many trillions of cells is irrelevant. A surviving cancerous cell will replicate itself, resulting in two cancerous cells. Two cancerous cells out of many trillions is still not a problem. As the cancerous cells continue to replicate, at some point the body takes note and mobilizes to destroy the cancer. This protective process is managed by cortisol.

CORTISOL

Cortisol is the action hormone, as well as the stress hormone. There are cortisol receptors in every cell of the body, implying its critical nature for human life. Cortisol helps regulate how resources are utilized in the body, which affects the immune system and how the body heals itself. Cortisol gushes into the bloodstream in two settings.

One is shortly after we awaken each morning. Cortisol floods the bloodstream, prompting the body to action to meet the day eagerly. This is why young children get up in the morning. Why should they? They have no goals or direction; they could stay in bed until noon or all day! Cortisol gushes into the bloodstream, and they're off and running!

The other time is when there is a threat or stressor (a Wolf). Cortisol floods the bloodstream, prompting the body to action to handle the stressor. If you get a cut on your hand, cortisol directs, "Clean up on aisle 9!" The body responds and begins diverting resources to deal with the problem, and your hand begins healing. If a Wolf suddenly appears, the message says, "Alert, Beware, Danger! Divert all resources toward dealing with the larger threat, the Wolf. Otherwise, we'll have a nicely healed hand in the casket!" The body will stop using resources to heal the hand and will use all available resources to survive the Wolf.

The body is designed to heal itself and deal with 'cuts.' Excessive stress interferes with this process, and the damage can then increase to unmanageable levels. Numerous studies are indicating that many debilitating illnesses come about due to stress and unprocessed emotion. This underscores the unmitigated significance of processing emotion proficiently!

> *Research indicates the human system is designed to handle a dozen or fewer Wolves a year. Many of us deal with multiple Wolves before breakfast!*

> *Stressors don't cause heart attacks; stress does.*

PSYCHOLOGICAL DISORDERS

Until a few years ago, psychological disorders were viewed in categories, e.g. you were psychotic or you were not, you were schizophrenic or you were not, you were autistic or you were not, etc. Research shows that psychological disorders exist on a spectrum, not in a category. While not all psychological disorder tests are standardized, the idea is that there are points from zero to a hundred. Whenever someone approaches eighty on such a scale, there is concern, as the individual struggles managing their behavior and life.

A psychological disorder is simply a disorder of the psyche, of the mind. Instead of a clear point A to point B thought process, the mind gets knocked off course. A mounting body of evidence indicates that many psychological disorders, including addictions, are facilitated or even caused by unprocessed emotion. The unprocessed emotion disorders behavior.

If someone clanged a metal pot beside you all day, pain would fire in the brain with increasing intensity, becoming unbearable. When you got home and your children exclaimed their excitement about your arrival, your brain would process that noise as pain, not joy. Because of the continuous pain experience of the day, your psyche would be disordered, and you would present a bad version of yourself. That's not because you are a bad person, but because of the emotional experience of the day (that stupid clanging pot). The pain experience of the day needs to be processed for the psyche to function in an orderly manner.

Everyone deals with some disorder of the psyche on some level, which is usually facilitated by unprocessed emotion. This underscores the significance of doing the Core Emotion Wheel every day (only four minutes) to retrain your brain to process emotion proficiently.

A note about addiction: Humans are coded to connect. It may be with work, hobbies, expenditures, substances, other humans or something else, but we will connect.

In the 1980s, Dr Bruce Alexander studied drug addiction. In a research project, he placed a rat in what he called Rat Park, where the rat's needs were provided, including a water bottle. Another water bottle laced with heroin was placed beside the plain water bottle. The individual rats always became addicted to heroin, with most of them overdosing and dying. Dr Alexander published research findings about the addictive properties of drugs such as heroin.

In examining his own research, he placed a *group* of rats in Rat Park. While some of the rats did occasionally drink from the heroin laced water, none became addicted, none overdosed and none died from overdosing. With the rats, the opposite of addiction was not sobriety. The opposite of addiction was connection. The same is true with humans.

Glenn:

In the late 1980s, I scored 84 out of 100 on an Obsessive Compulsive Disorder scale. I might accomplish in an hour what most people accomplished in ten minutes. It could take me a day to do what most people did in a couple of hours, etc. The money in my wallet was ironed and in serial number order. (That's why the serial numbers are on there!)

My clothes had to be on the 'correct' color hanger. The towels had to be folded with the tag placed correctly. (That's why they put tags on them, duh.) Oh, and make sure they're stacked perfectly. I avoid stepping on cracks. (You could trip or fall.) Opening a cereal box was a project to make sure the cardboard wasn't torn. The lost time led to my motto of "Work harder, not smarter." This was exhausting and extremely detrimental!

I score in the 50s and 60s on a number of other psychological disorder scales. As I have learned to process emotion proficiently, these disorders lose their power and grip, and I am able to function in an ordered manner. These disorders are ever present but not paralyzing, because I process the underlying emotion as it happens.

Phyllis:
I was clueless about what was happening with the guy I adored. The intense conflicts between us were endlessly disconnecting. I had no idea how to keep up with Glenn's preferences and systems or even what they were. Usually, our arguments would include Glenn saying, "If you loved me, you would do it this way." This bewildered me even more, as I knew I loved him and wasn't folding the towels a certain way because I did or didn't love him. Once we had children, I was just glad the laundry was done!

Several movies revealed insights that helped me get what was happening: As Good as it Gets, A Beautiful Mind *and* What About Bob. *Glenn is a genius, but I began to see how disordered his mind is because of unprocessed emotion that shuts down his cognition, resulting in him being an inferior version of himself. These movies had a huge effect on me, as I began to understand that Glenn does not ask for these things to happen in his psyche. He doesn't try to have these struggles. I realized what a burden he was carrying and began learning to partner with him in his experience.*

Glenn:

A woman who experienced a high level of arachnophobia came to my office. Her life had become dysfunctional and unproductive due to her struggle.

I could have conveyed the following and been correct:

- *The vast majority of spiders are not venomous.*
- *There is a considerably higher chance of dying in a car wreck than dying from a spider bite. (She had driven to my office.)*
- *Spiders avoid interaction with humans as much as possible. There are no attack spiders.*
- *Research indicates we are never more than six feet from a spider; there are spiders above*

ceilings and below floors everywhere. (There is a spider that lives in a Bonsai tree in my office- I did not tell her that.)

I could have proven to a judge and jury that the level of her fear was not 'appropriate' for the level of the threat. I would have won the court case but lost the relationship.

I realized she is not trying to experience fear; the emotion is happening to her. She may need to go over logistical information at some point, but if I resist her energy and respond with logistics (facts and figures, information...), she will shut down and not benefit from our relationship. By following her energy and being present with her, she was able to be safe, process her emotion, make progress in her struggle and become functional.

> *I can be who I need to be, when I'm free to be who I am.*

Glenn:

There are two types of people in the world: those who open cereal boxes correctly and those who do not. We have one of each in our marriage. For some reason, Phyllis is unable to experience enough joy to be prompted to open a cereal box cautiously and gently, you know- properly. She also is unable to experience pain when the cardboard on the cereal box is damaged. We don't know why this is true for her and *besides, Connection Coders don't ask why. I assume it's due to some sort of psychological disorder, as I am unable not to experience enough joy to be prompted to open a cereal box cautiously and gently, you know- properly. I also am unable not to experience pain when the cardboard on the cereal box is damaged.*

For many years, scenarios of this nature brought terrible conflict and disconnection for us. Now I am able to process my emotions, and we remain connected. I hope you get my facetiousness in the previous paragraph. We now are able to recognize the disorders with my psyche, and they have become entertaining, endearing and connecting for us!

CO-REGULATION

Research shows that co-regulation uses up to 80% less glucose than self regulation. Glucose is the fuel that powers the brain, and the brain directs the body.

CONSIDER

You've been getting 30 miles per gallon in your car. Suddenly you begin getting 150 mpg, and you tell your friend, "This is amazing! I filled up with gas nearly a month ago, and I still have a quarter of a tank left."

Conversely, you've been getting 30 mpg and suddenly you begin getting six mpg. You tell your friend, "This is awful! I filled up with gas yesterday morning, and I'm going to have to fill up again tomorrow.

This analogy is parallel to self versus co-regulation. When we self regulate, we use significantly more fuel than when we co-regulate. Dr Jim Coan in the Hand Holding experiments concluded that the fear and pain experience can be reduced up to 100% when shared with a trusted loved one. This is consistent with findings involving Lynne Cox in *Swimming in the Sink*, as well as David Tand's bioenergetic resource research. When we self regulate, we literally use more fuel, leaving us with less energy and power. When we co-regulate, we literally use less fuel, leaving us with more energy and power.

Glenn:

I am usually the last person to leave my office building each evening, frequently after dark. There is a group of people, some of them probably serial killers, who live in the bushes in the rear parking lot of my office building. While I lack evidence to support such a claim, I nonetheless remain convinced. I've never actually seen any of them, but I'm sure they're there. For years I would exit the building and speed up until I was safely inside my car with the doors locked. I would then rapidly drive away in a frantic effort to escape the pitchforks, machetes and chainsaws behind me. Sometimes I would burst into a sprint as I headed towards my car, certain that an extra second could be the difference between life and death.

I shared this with Phyllis one day, and she said, "Awww, Babe, that's awful. From now on, call me when you're leaving the building, and I'll stay on the phone with you while you're getting in your car."

Let's reason through this: I am on the phone with my wife, who is miles away. When she hears the carnage the attackers are visiting on me, what exactly can she do? Call 911, so the first responders can find my dismembered body? Color commentate my demise? Tell me she loves me as I pass on?

Or would the alleged assailants not bother me, because they know Phyllis is on the phone? "Dang it; we can't assault him now. He's on the phone, probably talking to his wife. Rats- another missed opportunity!"

There's nothing she could do to assist me in my time of catastrophic need.

Nonetheless . . . when I call her, my fear dissipates or never even begins! Now that's powerful!

Glenn (aka Papa):

We were keeping all our grandchildren overnight so their parents could go out. We were putting them to bed, which is a wonderfully special routine that Phyllis and I enjoy.

I was lying beside our five year old grandson. He is a high-energy, delightful little fellow, who gets about 29 hours out of each day. He was full of energy: wiggling, lifting his legs up in the air and flopping them back down. This was initially entertaining, except that it affected the other children. This went on for several minutes.

Grandson (suddenly rolling over to me): Papa, I feel sad.

Glenn (touching Grandson's arm): Oooo, what's happening with sad.

Grandson: I feel sad, cause I miss my mom.

Glenn (following the energy): Mmmm, yeah, I get that. She's so special. I miss her sometimes too.

Grandson: Papa, of course you miss her. She's your son.

(Our daughter, his mom, was eight months pregnant with a girl.)

Glenn: Well actually, she's my daughter, just like your baby sister will your parents' daughter, and you're going to be her big brother. You're going to be an amazing big brother. I'm so excited for her.

I blah-blahed a few more sentences then became aware of his steady breathing, as he had fallen asleep. The little guy's sadness would not let his body rest, because the emotion had not been processed. Once he processed it and co-regulated with me, he fell asleep quickly.

> *When I finally gave up trying to be competent, I became powerful.*

COMPASSIONATE TOUCH

Extensive research shows the significance and power of compassionate touch. Children require it for health and even survival. There is excessive documentation of the devastating effect for children who do not receive compassionate touch. Adults desperately need it as well.

As long as someone is not afraid of the person touching them, receiving compassionate touch actually makes cells and thus the body healthier. Among other things, cells become more permeable to water.

Also, compassionate touch releases oxytocin, reducing pain and fear in the brain. When there is relational connection, there is more compassionate touch; when there is relational disconnection, there is less compassionate touch. Connection and compassionate touch are reciprocal.

Humans are the least likely species on the planet to survive independently, but we're the *most* likely to thrive *inter*dependently. We are coded from birth for deep connection and functioning interdependently with each other. As we learn to connect more and more deeply, we become more powerful, individually and collectively, and develop into the best versions of ourselves!

SECTION 5 TAKEAWAYS

Psycholation is devastating to the human condition.

Cortisol regulates the immune system.

Unprocessed emotion facilitates debilitating illnesses and phycological disorders.

Psychological disorders exist on a spectrum, not in a category.

A psychological disorder is simply a disorder of the psyche.

Each of us deals with some psychological disorder.

The opposite of addiction is connection.

Co-regulation uses up to 80% less glucose than self regulation.

Compassionate touch and connection are reciprocal.

CO-REGULATION EXPERIENCE ASSIGNMENT

When there is a stressor, my first tendency is to

A time when I was in psycholation:

I tend towards psycholation when I

It helps me to turn to others more quickly when

CO-REGULATION EXPERIENCE ASSIGNMENT

When there is a stressor, my first tendency is to eat poorly and stop taking care of myself.

A time when I was in psycholation: When my company tripled in business over 3 months. I needed advice and help, and I didn't get it.

I tend towards psycholation when I feel fear of judgment.

It helps me to turn to others more quickly when I feel safe.

Section 5
Focus

Be aware of Psycholation. Co-regulate as often and as quickly as possible.

Notice when and how your psyche gets disordered.

Implement compassionate touch as often as possible.

Conclusion & Beginning

The Connection Codes are a way of life. They are the blueprint and tools for human connection. They are direct and implementable, allowing relationships to heal and develop to the deepest possible level. Implementing the Connection Codes creates a safe environment in which you can thrive and unleash your greatest potential!

This will be the most challenging thing you have ever done; it will also be the most rewarding. To continue your *Connection Codes* journey, follow us on Facebook and Instagram @connectioncodes. Visit connectioncodes.co for e-courses, private sessions and more.

You need this.
You deserve this.
Let's do this!

Dr Glenn Hill is a marriage and family therapist, clinical sexologist, Connection Codes coach and author with a private practice in Nashville, TN. He considers his greatest credential to be his 39-year marriage with Phyllis. He enjoys doing absolutely anything with her, especially traveling and spending time with their family of twenty.

Phyllis Hill is an entrepreneur, Connection Codes coach and the engine that keeps everything running. She enjoys the partnership and adventures she and Glenn share and loves being "Honey" to their ten grandchildren.

The pain of their early married years along with decades of research and experience led the Hills to the founding of The Connection Codes. They counsel couples, families, individuals, churches and businesses in building deep connection. They are passionate about the Connection Codes because of the effect on their relationship, as well as seeing the effect for countless others. It is the Hills' mission to take the Connection Codes to everyone on the planet.

Echo Vetter is Phyllis and Glenn's oldest child. She is a writer, Connection Codes coach, wife and homeschooling mom of five with a passion for mental health, women's health and helping families connect and thrive.

She does most of her reading and writing during long hikes and runs through the rolling hills near her home. She spends summers road tripping with her family, exploring, hiking and learning along the way.